DO YOU LOVE ME?

for Carolyn —
a friend who
loves our Lord.

Victor Shepherd

Lent 2008

DO YOU LOVE ME?

And Other Questions Jesus Asks

VICTOR SHEPHERD

CLEMENTS PUBLISHING
Toronto

Published 2007 by
Clements Publishing
213-6021 Yonge Street
Toronto, Ontario
M2M 3W2 Canada
www.clementspublishing.com

Library and Archives Canada Cataloguing in Publication

Shepherd, Victor A., 1944-
Do you love me? And other questions Jesus asked / Victor Shepherd.

ISBN-10: 1-894667-69-7
ISBN-13: 978-1-894667-69-2

1. Sermons, Canadian (English). I.Title.

BX9882.S48 2007   252   C2007-902616-8

CONTENTS

For Emmanuel Presbyterian Church, Schomberg,
on its
One Hundredth Anniversary

"...thankful for your partnership in the gospel..."
(Philippians 1:5)

INTRODUCTION

The first-time reader of the written gospels can't help noticing that Jesus never answers the question he's asked. The mother of James and John, for instance, asks Jesus to grant her two sons places of privileges in the Kingdom (Matthew 20:20-22). Jesus replies by posing his own question: "You do not know what you are asking. *Are you able to drink the cup that I am to drink?*"

In the same way the chief priests of the temple and the elders of the people ask Jesus, "By what authority are you doing these things, and who gave you this authority?" (Matthew 21:20). Again Jesus declines to answer their question but instead puts his question to them: "I also will ask you a question; and if you tell me the answer, then I also will tell you by what authority I do these things. *The baptism of John, whence was it? From heaven or from men?*"

Our Lord acts in this manner not because he disdains those who have come to him, and not because he relishes teasing seekers, let alone frustrating and even exasperating them. He declines to answer the question, rather, inasmuch as he knows it isn't the right question. Certainly they think it is. But that's because they are attempting to apprehend the truth of the Kingdom from a non-Kingdom standpoint. Jesus insists that only as they stand within the Kingdom—that is, only as the reality of the Kingdom radically relativizes all else—will they see their question to be inappropriate.

Our Lord grants this new angle-of-vision, this Kingdom-perspective, only as he uses their question as the occasion of his posing his question, the question they should have asked but couldn't. Having posed the proper question to them, the answer they give it—not merely with their lips but chiefly with their lives—will ultimately determine who they are before the Father.

We must understand that our questions are not dismissed as trite. Our questions are important. Our questions express the sincerest aspirations of our hearts. For this reason neither the questions nor questioners are disregarded. Yet since the sincerity of our hearts leaves us sincerely corrupt (Jeremiah 17:9), a new heart and new spirit (Ezekiel 18:31; 36:26) and a new mind (Romans 12:2) must be accorded us. The questions Jesus asked then and continues to ask now are the means whereby all of this happens.

The questions we bring to Jesus can be about anything at all. They are important not because they are the profoundest but because they are the occasion of our proximity to him. Once in his orbit, we find our questions taken up in his gracious purposes for us, as our questions lend him opportunity to address himself to us, even give himself to us—while his questions are the God-given opportunity of abandoning ourselves to him.

1

DO YOU LOVE ME?

When they had finished breakfast, Jesus said to Simon Peter, "Simon, son of John, do you love me more than these?" He said to him, "Yes, Lord; you know that I love you." He said to him, "Feed my lambs." A second time he said to him, "Simon, son of John, do you love me?" He said to him, "Yes, Lord; you know that I love you." He said to him, "Tend my sheep." He said to him the third time, "Simon, son of John, do you love me?" Peter was grieved because he said to him the third time, "Do you love me?" And he said to him, "Lord, you know everything; you know that I love you." Jesus said to him, "Feed my sheep. Truly, truly, I say to you, when you were young, you girded yourself and walked where you would; but when you are old, you will stretch out your hands, and another will gird you and carry you where you do not wish to go." (This he said to show by what death he was to glorify God.) And after this he said to him, "Follow me."

—John 21:15-19

What do people do when they are let down terribly? What do people do when they suffer enormous loss and are bereaved beyond telling? They can do several things.

They can deny their loss; i.e., consciously deny the significance of their loss or unconsciously deny the fact of their loss. They can put on a false face and pretend that everything is as rosy as ever. Conscious and unconscious denial, however, exact a terrible price psychologically. Denial renders people inwardly bent and outwardly lame.

Or people who suffer enormous loss can simply be overwhelmed by it; so overwhelmed as to be frozen, immobilised by it; life stops for them. This is a living death.

Or people who suffer enormous loss can admit their loss, own their pain and endure their disappointment. They can admit, own, endure, and go back to work. They can begin doing once more whatever it is they have customarily done. The job they have worked at they continue to work at. This is by far the healthiest response. It's the best thing that any bereaved person can do.

My wife Maureen and I often comment on the fact that when my mother was Maureen's age my mother had been a widow for eleven years. At the time she was widowed my mother was working part-time and was content to work part-time. One week after my father's death, however, she was working full-time. My father had left her an insurance payout of $1000 (1967). After funeral expenses she had $200. The decision to work full-time was a decision my mother arrived at quickly after little deliberation: if she didn't work, she didn't eat. She often joked about riding the subway train to work, packed so tightly into the rush-hour car that if she had fainted she couldn't have fallen down, her face pressed into the back of a tall man's rain-soaked woollen overcoat, everything smelling like wet dog. She also says that what she *had* to do was the best thing she *could* have done: work.

And this is what the disciples did in the wake of the death of Jesus. They went back to fishing. They had been rocked by the events in the last week of Jesus's life, shattered by the ending of that life. Worst of all, they felt themselves deluded, self-deluded, as gullible as kindergarten-age children. "How could we have been so naïve?" they asked each other incredulously; "Our earlier enthusiasm for the mission was as groundless as a mirage in the desert. How could we have been so simple-minded, so silly about 'The Messiah'? We aren't suggestible people. Then how were we swept up in the tide of exuberance and ardour? Worse still, how many others have we misled? How ardently have we commended to any who would hear us what has dribbled away without trace like water in the sand?"

All of us are eager to think ourselves sophisticated. We hate being suckered as we hate little else. All of us like to think we are worldly-wise, able to identify hucksters and charlatans and outright phoneys. We shudder at being thought as naïve as a child standing wide-eyed and open-mouthed in front of a magician. There's no humiliation like the humiliation of an incredulity that's publicly observable.

And there's no humiliation like the humiliation of being taken in religiously. Who doesn't feel sorry for the person who, perchance at a moment of unusual need or unforeseen vulnerability, makes a religious declaration that strikes us as hugely overblown or espouses a religious cause that's plainly exaggerated? We share the embarrassment of that person who, months later, feels she "went off the deep end." What do such people do next? If they are wise they put their embarrassment behind them and simply get on with the business of everyday living.

A minute ago I spoke of bereavement, of loss. We mustn't think that jarring loss is loss of loved one only. There are bereavements everywhere in life. There are familiar scenarios and situations that are so very familiar as to appear impossible to lose. But they *are* lost nonetheless. Not merely a familiar scenario and situation can be lost but even a familiar *world*. Someone's entire world can be lost, and lost more quickly and more thoroughly than she would ever have thought—than she would ever have thought, that is, until the day it *was* lost. She always thought she knew how the world turned and what made it turn. Then one day she found out. The day she found out—the day of her shattering disappointment—was also the day she was bereft of her world.

Denial won't help. Immobility won't help. The only thing to do is also the best thing to do: go back to work. If our work is the work of a homemaker, it's still work: children have to be fed, the schoolteacher dealt with, the haemorrhaging husband bandaged.

"I'm going fishing," said Peter; "We'll go with you," the rest chimed in; "What else is there to do?" Back to fishing they went.

* * * * *

It's while they are fishing that Jesus appears to them. They don't recognise him. This should be no surprise. In the first place, they aren't expecting him; in the second, they're fishing. None of us can be conscientious in our daily work and be looking for Jesus at the same time. Besides, where would we look? The men and women who tighten wheel nuts on cars in Oakville or Oshawa or pour molten steel in Hamilton aren't standing around, looking for Jesus.

Still, despite all non-expectations the risen Lord steals upon the disciples and startles them. He speaks. As he speaks, Peter recognises the One he'd put behind him forever—he thought.

It still happens. The late William Sloane Coffin, among other things chaplain at Yale University for 17 years, and before that an officer with United States military intelligence; Coffin was raised by a wealthy, socialite family that recognised his prodigious talent as a child pianist and prepared him for a career on the concert stage. His family provided no Christian formation at all. When Coffin was an adolescent his best friend died suddenly. Coffin wasn't sure why he was going to the funeral, but went anyway, if only to curse the God he didn't believe in. Sitting through the funeral service he mysteriously found himself addressed: "Whose life is it, anyway? What makes you think you're the measure of the universe?" He emerged from the funeral service turned around for life, retiring a few years ago as minister of Riverside Church, New York City.

The parents of a friend of mine couldn't get their teenaged son to church regardless of what technique they deployed. At the close of his adolescence my friend—atheist, sceptic, cynic—went to university to pursue an Honours program in English. Naturally enough his program required him to read English criticism, including criticism of mediaeval English. Scholars in this field opened up literary riches to him, cultural wealth he hadn't known to exist. One such scholar was C. S. Lewis, Cambridge Professor of Mediaeval and Renaissance English. Soon he moved from reading Lewis's formal academic writings to Lewis's popular Christian writings. And like Peter of old he came to say, "It is the Lord."

Neither of the two men I've mentioned was expecting any such thing. Both were immersed in everyday matters. Yet both were addressed. In the course of being addressed both came to know who had addressed them.

The apostle John adds a comment to his resurrection narrative in John 21: "This was the third time that Jesus was revealed to the disciples after he was raised from the dead." The third time? Why was a third time necessary? Weren't the previous two times enough? First the risen Jesus had appeared to the eleven in the upper room when they were fearful. Then he had appeared to them with Thomas when they were doubt-saturated. And after two such appearances the disciples *still* want to go back fishing? The truth is, all of us always stand in need of a new visitation from our Lord and a new word from him. We never get beyond needing yet another apprehension and word.

DO YOU LOVE ME?

My wife and I have been married for 39 years. Even so, a dozen times a week we ask each other, "Do you love me?" I don't think for a minute we are insecure in our relationship. I don't think for a minute that our marriage is at risk and I might go home one evening only to find that Maureen has fled the marital home. Then why do we ask each other "Do you love me?" as often as we do? It's because both she and I live and work in jarring, turbulent environments where it's easy to see there are many people who *aren't* loved; easy to see there are many people who were *once* loved; easy to see that love is scarce in the world. Therefore it's all the more important to meet each other yet again, affirm each other once more, declare and exhibit and embody our mutual love as often as we need to; better, as often as we can.

We shouldn't be surprised at the *third* appearance of Jesus. Before you and I are finished our Lord will have to visit us 300 times. Needy as we are, our need is never greater than his grace.

* * * * *

Yet our Lord does more than visit us again and renew our life with him once more. He also puts a question to us, the same question he put to Peter: "Do you love me more than these?" The Greek word for love that Jesus uses here is strong: it's love in the sense of total self-giving, total self-outpouring, thorough self-forgetfulness, utter self-abandonment. It's the word used of God himself, for God so *loved* the world that he gave—himself, utterly, without remainder or regret—in his Son.

"Do you love me like *that*," the master says to Peter; "Do you love me more than these other fellows love me?" Now Peter is shaken. His fellow disciples were present, one week earlier, when Peter told Jesus that *these fellows* might crumble, cowards, when the crunch came, but he, Peter, the rock, would remain steadfastly loyal, brave and true. Then *these fellows* saw Peter fall all over himself. Now they are watching him. So shaken is Peter that he can't answer the master's question. He can only blurt, head down, "You know that I love you."

15

The English translations of our Bible hide something crucial: Peter doesn't use the same word for "love" that Jesus has used. Peter uses a weaker word. Jesus has said, "Are you willing to sign yourself over to me, abandon yourself to me, never looking back?" Peter is nervous now about vowing anything this large, since the last time he vowed something large he disgraced himself. Now Peter can only reply cautiously, "You know that I'm fond of you; you know that I care for you."

Jesus asks a second time, "Do you love me?", using again the strongest word for love that there is. Now Peter is in pain. As if his pain weren't enough, he's asked a third time, "Do you love me?"—only this time Jesus uses the word of Peter's earlier reply, Peter's weaker word. "Simon, are you truly fond of me? Do you really care for me? If this is as much as you can honestly say, will you say this much?" Peter replies, "You know everything; you know that I care for you." After each question and answer Jesus says to Peter, "Feed my sheep." It's a commission, an invitation and a promise: "Feed my sheep."

We are and continue to be disciples not because of superior insight or unusual loyalty or extraordinary grip on Jesus Christ. Like Peter we are disciples only because our Lord keeps coming to us, keeps speaking to us, and continues to hold us with a grip greater than our grip on him. And when he says "Do you love me?" we don't jump up and say, "Of course we do. Isn't it obvious? Could anyone doubt it?" We don't say this because, like Peter, we've heard the rooster crow. Instead we barely manage to croak, but do manage to croak, "You know that I care for you." Never shall we find him saying "Not good enough; see me in six months." Always he will say "Feed my sheep."

None of this means we are patently discouraged or depressed or immobilised or even suffering from low self-esteem. On the contrary, the master's question, "Do you love me?", *plus* his commission, "Feed my sheep," are a double safeguard. In the first place we are safeguarded against spiritual presumption. "Of course we love you. Our faith is proverbial, our obedience faultless, our life exemplary." The question Jesus puts to us repeatedly just because he *has* to put it to us repeatedly; this question spares us a spiritual presumptuousness as repugnant as it is false.

At the same time his commission, "Feed my sheep," reinforced relentlessly, safeguards us against despondency and uselessness. He has promised that whatever we do in obedience to him; whatever we undertake in his name will become food for his sheep. We aren't asked to be super-achievers or heroic or even merely impressive; we need only be faithful, and our faithfulness, even when pot-holed like Peter's, he will yet use to expand his own life within his own people. For our Lord's commission, "Feed my sheep," is more than a commission; it's more even than an invitation; it's a promise: we *can* feed his sheep, and we *shall*, just because he, unlike us, keeps the promises he makes.

The last word to Peter is, Follow me. To *follow* our risen Lord means that he asks us to go only where he has already been himself. He asks us to do only what he has already done himself. He asks us to intercede on behalf of the world only as he has already interceded on its behalf himself. To *follow* him means that we are never appointed to a work whose venue and environment he hasn't already prepared for us. To *follow* him means that he's forever drawing us to himself, never driving us on ahead of him. To *follow* him means that our obedience always decreases the distance between him and us; only our disobedience can ever increase the distance. To *follow* him means that his word of pardon and freedom and encouragement is a much louder word and a more penetrating sound than the raucous screech of the rooster. To *follow* is simply to know that our Lord will ever use us to feed others in ways that we cannot see and don't have to see.

He who appeared to disciples so very long ago with a word, a question and a promise will continue to come to you and me. His word will let us recognise him. His question will save us from any suggestion of superiority. And his promise, "Feed my sheep," will ensure that we do just that.

2

BUT WHO DO YOU SAY THAT I AM?

Now when Jesus came into the district of Caesare'a Philippi, he asked his disciples, "Who do men say that the Son of man is?" And they said, "Some say John the Baptist, others say Eli'jah, and others Jeremiah or one of the prophets." He said to them, "But who do you say that I am?" Simon Peter replied, "You are the Christ, the Son of the living God." And Jesus answered him, "Blessed are you, Simon Bar-Jona! For flesh and blood has not revealed this to you, but my Father who is in heaven. And I tell you, you are Peter, and on this rock I will build my church, and the powers of death shall not prevail against it. I will give you the keys of the kingdom of heaven, and whatever you bind on earth shall be bound in heaven, and whatever you loose on earth shall be loosed in heaven." Then he strictly charged the disciples to tell no one that he was the Christ.

—Matthew 16:13-20

I wince whenever I hear jokes about the mainline churches that appear to have become "sideline." I wince for several reasons: one, it's painful to have to watch a large denomination decline day after day; two, the mainline denominations began centuries ago with great promise as they exalted the gospel and magnified Jesus Christ and endeavoured to meet human need; three, I still hold out hope for the mainline denominations. Dr. Ian Rennie, a Presbyterian minister (now retired) who used to be academic dean of my seminary; Ian Rennie told me he prayed every day for the reinvigoration of The United Church of Canada. "I pray every day for the revival of faith within the Canadian nation," he said, "and in light of the place The United Church occupies in our nation, revival can appear in Canada only as The United Church is revitalized."

For thirty years The United Church was the fastest declining denomination in Canada, its book membership today being virtually what its book membership was when it was formed in 1925. The other mainline denominations are in no less grave a predicament.

Of course the haemorrhage can always be made to appear less frightening. Figures can be juggled to ease the shock; altering year book totals, for instance, to include *all* the families on any military base where a denomination has one chaplain. It's all reminiscent of Admiral Nelson's order to have the decks of his warships painted blood red; that way, in the heat of battle sailors would be slower to recognize and be shocked at the blood of shipmates pouring over the decks.

From time to time I hear nervous denominational leaders quoting Christ's promise to Peter: "On this rock I will build my church, and the powers of death will never triumph over it." They quote the promise, seemingly assuming that the promise guarantees the preservation of an institution.

And they are wrong. Our Lord has promised no such thing. His promise—always to be counted on—was never made to an organization. His promise, rather, guarantees that he will ever cherish, protect and preserve his people, his followers, his community, his fellowship. He will protect and preserve the fellowship that looks to him and clings to him in the midst of an unbelieving world. We shouldn't think, however, that this means he's going to preserve any denomination. History is littered with the dry bones of long-dead congregations and denominations.

We have to keep reminding ourselves that we can't coast on the faith and faithfulness of our foreparents. "Everyone must do his own believing," Luther liked to say, "just as everyone must do his own dying." History indicates that as the Spirit of God brings to birth a new manifestation of the people of God, the church—eager, ardent, compassionate, self-renouncing—this new manifestation has about one and a half generations before it slides into "Let's coast on our grandparents", only to find that it can't.

Francis of Assisi melted hearts as he and his band of men revitalized the church through their cheerful evangelism (despite the romantic depiction of Assisi as a nature-mystic we should always keep in mind that he was chiefly an evangelist) and through their self-forgetful service. One hundred and fifty years later Franciscan friars were notorious for their greed, their corruption, their lechery. When Franciscans appeared in a village parents kept their daughters indoors.

John Wesley and his followers flared into a purifying fire that Anglicanism could neither welcome nor douse. Yet within seventy years of Wesley's death Methodism had grown so cold, so callous, so spiritually inert that Methodism couldn't accommodate William Booth, founder of the Salvation Army.

Christians of every generation are slow to hear that God has no grandchildren. God certainly has children: we become God's children as we seize Jesus Christ in faith and vow never to let go. Grandchildren, however, are those who try to ride on the coattails of their parents' faith, sooner or later to find that what they assumed to be possible—faith at arm's length, faith second-hand, faith on the cheap—isn't possible.

Jesus Christ puts the same questions to every generation. His community lives and thrives only as it answers these questions for itself in every generation.

* * * * *

One of the many questions that our Lord puts to us is, "Who do you say that I am? Never mind what anyone else is saying; who do *you* say that I am?" When the first disciples were addressed they gave the answers that they were hearing all around them, answers that they overheard others proffer. "Some people say you are Elijah all over again." Elijah was to herald God's new age. "Some people say you are John the Baptist." John had fearlessly urged repentance on his hearers. "Some people say you are a prophet." A prophet announces God's judgement as well as God's mercy and the future that only God can give his people. "Never mind what 'they' are saying," replies Jesus; "it's time for you to answer for yourselves. Who do *you* say that I am?" Voicing the conviction of the twelve Peter cries, "You are the Christ, the Son of the living God."

To be the Son of God is to possess the nature of God. And to possess the nature of God is to incarnate God's purpose, God's will. When Jesus pronounces the paralysed man forgiven, critics accuse him, "But only God can forgive sin." "You're right", says Jesus; "only God can forgive sin, and I have just forgiven it. Either I'm the crudest blasphemer or I speak and act uniquely with the authority of God himself. Now which is it?" Months later Thomas will cry out in the midst of confusion and frustration, "Just show us the Father and it will be enough." Jesus will reply, "To see *me* is to see the *Father.*"

We who are disciples of Jesus Christ are not unitarians. We do not believe that the truth, the decisive truth, the whole truth is told about Jesus when he is said to be a helpful teacher and a moral guide. The Church has never been built on the suggestion that Jesus is the high point of humankind's aspiration after the good, the true and the beautiful. We do not believe that Jesus is the lucky winner in that treasure hunt that is sometimes called "The Human Search for God." The community of disciples doesn't arise from a public admission that Jesus is a spiritual genius, the random development in the religious world that Mozart was in the musical world.

Without denying the humanness of Jesus in any way; without denying the fact that from a human perspective Jesus was a child of his times in many respects, disciples of Jesus yet are constrained to cry with Thomas when Thomas looked upon the crucified one raised and exclaimed, "My Lord and my God."

Thomas's cry and confession is a rebuke to the doctrinal slovenliness of so many denominational statements. Recently I was given a pamphlet on worship stating that worship is chiefly a matter of feeling good about ourselves. Worship isn't this at all. Worship is giving public expression to the unsurpassable worthiness of God. Surely we are weary of receiving Christian Education literature at Christmas time telling us that the purpose of Christ's coming was "to tell us that God loves us", as though lack of information were the root human problem. The root human problem isn't lack of information, ignorance of the truth that God loves us; the root human problem is a corrupted heart. The good news of great joy that thrilled early-day Christians was that they'd been given a Saviour; a Saviour, not an encyclopaedia.

Doctrinal slovenliness always breeds ethical confusion. It's no wonder we're told that the life of a murderer is so precious before God that it mustn't be taken, while the life of the pre-born child is so insignificant that it needn't be protected. This kind of confusion is the outcome of the those who are doctrinally indifferent and who cavalierly dismiss Peter's confession, "You are the Son of the living God."

"Peter said more than this," someone reminds us. Indeed, Peter said, "You are *the Christ; i.e., the anointed One, the Messiah*, the Son of the living God." Ever since Isaiah 53—"he was wounded for our transgressions, he was bruised for our iniquities, like a lamb that is led to the slaughter..."—ever since Isaiah 53, discerning Israelites who knew God's way and will knew that to be an obedient servant of God would always entail harassment and suffering. Peter knew this.

Yet Jesus seemed so alive, so fresh, so full of life that he appeared indestructible. Jesus had to be an exception. Other servants of God may be set upon, but not *the* servant. Surely the Messiah is here to end human distress, not become another victim of it. Peter argues in this way with Jesus until Jesus finally shouts at him, "Satan! You, Peter, are satanic." Satan is the one who frustrates God's work. Satan is the deceiver. Plainly Jesus is telling Peter that not to acknowledge him, Jesus, as *suffering* Messiah is to deceive oneself and to frustrate the work of God. Jesus speaks to Peter as harshly as he does because he can't allow his disciples to persist in a misunderstanding that misleads God's people and impedes God's work.

Jesus isn't finished with the twelve. After he has jarred them by insisting that he's no exception to Isaiah 53, he jars them again by telling them that *they* are no exception. "If you want to be my disciple," he insists without qualification, "you must deny yourself, take up your cross and follow me." Followers of Jesus simply can't avoid self-renunciation. For being a disciple means that we both cling to him as Son of God and identify ourselves with that Messianic community whose self-renunciation is quickened by self-renunciation of the Messiah himself. These two aspects are welded inseparably together.

The six-million-dollar fence on Toronto's Bloor Street Viaduct will prevent more people from leaping to their death. Four hundred and fifty have done so already. My sister is a volunteer in a program that provides assistance for people who are distressed on account of sudden, untoward disruption: car accident, house fire, drowning, suicide, etc.

On one occasion my sister had spent the night bringing what comfort she could to a 28-year-old fellow who was tormented by what he had seen that afternoon. He had been driving across the Bloor Viaduct when he noticed a man standing on the railing with a rope around his neck. Immediately the young fellow wheeled his car around in a "U-turn," leapt out and ran towards the man on the railing—who jumped off the Viaduct at that moment.

Until my mother was felled by a major heart attack she belong to the same assistance program. At age 70 my mother often headed out into the night to sit with someone she had never seen before, someone whose house had caught fire or whose husband had died at work or whose child was missing. My parents lived in Edmonton for eleven years (1938-1949), and during that eleven-year period my father visited convicts in Fort Saskatchewan Penitentiary *every Sunday afternoon*. I grew up in a family that knew that discipleship always entails self-denial.

For this reason I was all the more stunned on my first pastoral charge when I stumbled upon a government facility in Chatham, NB (now the city of Miramichi.) My congregation was located forty miles from Chatham; I went in and out of the town principally to visit parishioners who were occasionally hospitalized there. One day I walked around town instead of getting into my car and heading home, only to come upon a large residence that housed intellectually challenged adults whose I.Q. was 55 (more or less.) With an I.Q. of 55 they could be toilet trained (you need 20 for that); they could be taught to thread beads on a string or cut up panty-hose and hook a rug. But of course they were never going to be gainfully employed. Unemployble and defenceless, they were also harmless. I entered the residence and workshop. Icily a staff worker stared at me and hissed, "We have been operating five months now and you are the first clergyman to appear in this facility." When she had recovered her composure she told me that upon hearing that the government planned to accommodate these developmentally challenged adults in Chatham, townspeople (church people included) had circulated petitions throughout the town asking the government to locate these disadvantaged persons somewhere else, *anywhere else*. She also told me what joy and what help church groups could have brought to these people: musical entertainment, dancing, men to kick around a soccer ball with residents, women to bake with female residents. I visited the facility once a week thereafter and discovered that I had as large a ministry to the staff as I had to the residents.

At the next meeting of the Ministerial Association I said gently, "There happens to be a facility in this town full of people whom the world disdains, together with a staff whose work no one appreciates—and it seems the local clergy don't care." Gently I commented on the town's attempts at disbarring wounded people who, unlike most of us, can't speak for themselves. The chair of the ministerial association called for the next item on the agenda.

To be a disciple is to cling to the One who is uniquely *the* Son of the living God, the suffering, self-renouncing Messiah. To cling to him, therefore, will always be to deny ourselves in a self-renunciation born of his as we are found in that Messianic community which knows and loves and obeys the Messiah himself.

* * * * *

What finally comes of it all? Jesus promises that the keys of the kingdom are entrusted to the community that is unashamed of its Lord and unhesitating in its self-renunciation.

What are the "keys of the kingdom"? Do we have magical power? Does it mean that we (or at least some of us, perhaps the clergy) have commandant-like authority whereby we can decide who is admitted to the kingdom and who not? Of course not. It means that the ongoing event of the congregation's faith and faithfulness and self-renunciation are precisely what Jesus Christ uses as the instrument of his bringing others to know and cherish what he has already brought us to know and cherish. Our lived awareness of his forgiveness, for instance, will be the event whereby he brings others to delight in the same reality. Our self-renunciation will be the means of his bringing others, now fellow-disciples like us, to know the "open secret": service is freedom, self-forgetfulness is self-fulfilment, crossbearing binds us to the crucified One himself whom we have come to know to be *life*. As we have stepped through the doorway into the household of faith, other people will find through our faith and obedience and service the same doorway unlocked, and shall then run to join us on the way.

The symbolism of Scripture is endlessly rich, so very rich that many different symbols are used to speak of the same reality. Instead if thinking about doorways and keys, let's think about boats. In Mark's gospel there's a great deal of water, and Jesus is always getting into and out of a boat. (The boat is an early Christian symbol for the Church, and was widely used as a symbol by the time Mark's gospel was written—65 C.E., approximately.) *In Mark's gospel, only Jesus and the disciples are ever found together in the boat.* The crowds, the "multitudes," are never found in the boat. In other words, there is a special relationship, a unique relationship between Jesus and his followers. At the same time the boat, rowed by the disciples, "conveys" Jesus to the crowds who aren't disciples at present but have been appointed to become disciples. The boat (the church) conveys Jesus to the deranged man whom Jesus restores. The boat conveys Jesus to the hungry listeners whom he feeds. The boat conveys Jesus to the agitated and perplexed whom he describes as "sheep without a shepherd" even as he becomes their good shepherd.

To be given the keys of the kingdom is the same as being used by our Lord to row the boat that carries *him* into the midst of those who are on their way to becoming disciples.

* * * * *

I have never doubted Christ's promise, "I will build my Church, and the powers of death shall never submerge it."

I have never doubted the confession to which the promise is made, "You—alone—are the Christ, the Messiah, the Son of the living God."

And I have never doubted the commitment that must accompany the confession, "If anyone wants to be my disciple, let her deny herself, renounce herself, take up her cross, follow me, and never look back."

3

WHY DO YOU CALL ME 'LORD, LORD,' AND NOT DO WHAT I TELL YOU?

"Why do you call me 'Lord, Lord,' and not do what I tell you? Every one who comes to me and hears my words and does them, I will show you what he is like: he is like a man building a house, who dug deep, and laid the foundation upon rock; and when a flood arose, the stream broke against that house, and could not shake it, because it had been well built. But he who hears and does not do them is like a man who built a house on the ground without a foundation; against which the stream broke, and immediately it fell, and the ruin of that house was great."

—Luke 6:46-49

At one time I was a postgraduate student at the University of Aberdeen, Scotland. Several of us offshore doctoral students were drinking coffee in a common room. We were comparing notes as to what we had had to do when we entered Great Britain. The students from the USA had had to check in with the police department. I hadn't had to, I said, inasmuch as I was a British subject.

"British *subject*," one of the American students exploded, "How can you admit to being a subject of any sort? Even if you are one you shouldn't use the word. It's demeaning." But I have never felt demeaned through being a British subject. I have never felt oppressed or cramped or belittled in any way. On the contrary I have always felt extraordinarily rich in being a British subject. After all, to be a British subject is to belong to the oldest democratic tradition in the world. Because it's the oldest, it's the most trustworthy. (To what extent would we trust the democratic "tradition" of the nations that are brand new democracies?) What's more, it was Britain that first insisted that no one could be jailed without being charged and convicted. It was Britain whose treatment of peoples subdued in military conflict was the gentlest. (Can you imagine where Quebec would be today if New France had succumbed to the Spanish or the Dutch?) Surely it's a privilege to be a British subject. The American student, on the other hand, thought it demeaning. Opinions were sharply divided.

33

* * * * *

Opinions are divided in the same way when God's claim upon our obedience is mentioned.

"Obedience", someone snorts, "Obedience is demeaning. 'Obedience' is another word for slavery and misery. You've got to be your own person, subject to no one."

The Christian disciple, on the other hand, knows that to hear the claim of God, to recognize the claim of God, to obey the claim of God—in short, to be subject to God—is a wonderful privilege that brings blessings. So who is right?

Whether God's claim upon our obedience enslaves or liberates depends on the root human condition. As though it were yesterday I remember sitting on a park bench in downtown Toronto (it was outside St. James Cathedral) before my wife, Maureen, and I were married. Maureen was an agnostic in those days, probably an atheist. She wasn't going to be stampeded into Christian "faith", if she was going to move into it at all. "I don't want to look at the world and life through spectacles (Christian faith) that only distort and falsify", she said. As gently as I could (there was a great deal at stake for me here) I explained that her unconscious assumption plainly was that humankind, *in its present condition*, has perfect eyesight, a true view of life; and therefore spectacles of any sort, but especially religious spectacles, necessarily distort and falsify. Yet according to the gospel, humankind has a heart condition and a head condition that together produce defective eyesight, terribly defective eyesight. In fact it is only as we put on Jesus Christ in faith—i.e., only as we put on the corrective lens that he is—that we see truly, see profoundly, and therefore see adequately.

To put on Christ is always to put on *all* of him: to put him on as saviour or salvager, also as companion and judge, and certainly as Lord. In other words, to be a disciple is to obey. There's genuine faith only where there's eager obedience. Where there isn't even aspiration to obedience then faith, so-called, is nothing more than sentimentality. For this reason

34

Jesus poses the question starkly, "Why do you call me 'Lord, Lord,' yet you don't *do* what I tell you?"

It has all come to our attention too many times over with the television preachers and others like them. Some people are terribly disillusioned by the disclosures; some are disgusted; some are angry. I'm sad more than anything else; sad that anyone is so very self-deceived as to think that disciples can disregard their Lord's claim upon them while remaining disciples.

* * * * *

In all of this few appear to understand a profound truth that is found everywhere in Scripture: obedience means freedom. The obedient person—and only the obedient person—is the free person. To grasp this, however, we have to understand how scripture understands freedom.

Most people think that freedom is having several alternatives to choose from. A young person goes to an ice cream parlour and finds that there are twenty-seven flavours available. Just imagine: twenty-seven, and she need choose only one. "What freedom," she thinks, meaning, "How fortunate I am to have so many choices." We all know what happens next. "I think I'll have strawberry ripple; I mean Swiss chocolate; no, tiger tail. Do you have any liquorice and peanut butter?" What the child calls "freedom"—one choice among twenty-seven—is really *indeterminism*. No one is twisting the girl's arm to pick a flavour. No one is determining which ice cream cone she is going to buy. Her situation isn't characterized by *freedom* but rather by *indeterminism*; that is, no power external to her is coercing her.

When the Bible speaks of freedom, however, it means something entirely different; it means *the absence of any impediment to acting in accord with our true nature.* Our true nature is to be a child of God by faith, and to reflect the family-resemblance found in Jesus our elder brother. The free person is simply the person for whom there is no

35

impediment (outer or inner), no obstacle to her living as the child of God that she is by faith.

As a disciple of Jesus Christ I'm not "free" in the sense that I can choose among many alternatives; I'm not "free" because I can choose to be honest, or semi-honest, or completely dishonest. I'm not "free" in the sense that I can choose to be joyfully faithful to my wife, grudgingly faithful to her, or out-and-out promiscuous. I'm not "free" in the sense that I can choose to be kind or indifferent or outright cruel. To be sure, I *can* choose among all the alternatives I've just listed. But choosing from a list of alternatives has nothing to do with freedom. Freedom means that I have been liberated from any impediment to living as a disciple of Jesus Christ. I have been *freed* from obstacles that would otherwise derail my discipleship. I may and do live as what I am: a child of God, recognizable from my likeness (however slight) to my elder brother.

Think for a minute of a railway train. Imagine that obstacles litter the track (say, a dump truck with granite slabs spilling out of it.) Since the obstacles are an impediment, the train isn't free to run along the track. Once the obstacles are removed, however, the train is free. "But is the train free to fly like an airplane?" someone wants to say. The question, be it noted, entails a misuse of the word "free." After all, trains were never meant to fly like airplanes; it isn't a train's nature to fly. It's a train's nature to run along tracks. Therefore a train has been freed when it is free to operate in accord with its own nature. All of which is to say that we are free when we cling to our Lord in faith and obey him in matters great and small and know ourselves children of our Father who reflect the family-resemblance of our elder brother. For then we are living in accord with our true nature. Obedience can only mean freedom. Freedom, in the biblical sense, isn't freedom *of* choice but profoundly freedom *from* choice.

* * * * *

All of which brings us to the last point. *Our blessedness is found in obedience.* So far from being a straitjacket that ties us up in frustration and self-contradiction and futility—curse, in short—obedience spells blessings. We are reminded of this every time we read a favourite psalm, Psalm 119. It's the longest chapter in all of scripture; and in every line it exalts the blessedness that accompanies obedience. The expression in Psalm 119 that we must linger over is the psalmist's cry that Torah, God's claim upon our obedience, is *sweeter than honey.*

When Jewish youngsters first learn the Hebrew alphabet, they are helped to do so by playing with wooden blocks into one side of which there has been carved a Hebrew letter. The letter-surface is coated with honey, and as the children learn the letters they get to lick the honey. For the rest of their lives they will know that the Hebrew language is sweet; and not only the language, but also Torah, God's truth and God's way that are described by the Hebrew language, the way that God has appointed Israel to walk. God's way—i.e., obedience—is sweeter than honey.

In the Hebrew Bible *yoke* is the commonest metaphor for obedience. Doesn't Jesus say, "Take my yoke upon you, for my yoke is easy and my burden is light"? His yoke fits well just because it and we have been made for each other. Since Christ's yoke doesn't gall or chafe, it's truly said to be "easy." And since his burden is so very light as to be no burden at all, his "burden" is actually blessing.

Yet how few people understand this. When most people think of the concrete, everyday obedience that God requires of us they think of the Ten Commandments. The mere sound of the word "commandment" puts them off, because the sound of the word suggests a parade-square sergeant barking at them. But is the atmosphere surrounding our obedience to our Father that of a barking parade-square sergeant? Or is it that of the delighted child who learns that Torah, life's alphabet, God's way, really is sweeter than honey?

Concerning the Ten Commandments Martin Luther wrote, "Whoever keeps the first (the commandment to have no other gods) keeps them all; whoever breaks the tenth (the commandment forbidding coveting) breaks them all." In not coveting at all—nothing of the neighbour's possessions, money, spouse, children, reputation or good fortune—we are blessed. Luther's reasoning is sound. If we covet our neighbour's goods, we thieve; if his reputation, we slander; if her spouse, we commit adultery; if her popularity or power, we murder. Plainly Luther was right: to break the commandment that forbids coveting is to break them all.

Needless to say, if obedience spells blessing then disobedience spells curse. Is this really the case? Let's look again at coveting. Insofar as we covet what someone else has we shall first be profoundly and pervasively discontented ourselves; next we shall resent her for having what we don't have; next we shall exaggerate character defects in her or even invent them; finally we shall want nothing to do with her for any number of supposedly good reasons, all of which are actually the crudest, albeit unconscious, rationalizations thrown up by our envious heart. Insofar as we covet we shall be consumed with envy of her, resentment at her, contempt for her and hostility toward her. At the end of it all we shall be left friendless, isolated, stuck with our own embittered spirit. Is there any freedom here? There *is* misery and frustration and nastiness. But is there any freedom, any blessing? There's curse, and curse alone. On the other hand, to obey the command of God from our heart is to know blessing. Then the apostle John is correct when he says, "God's commandments are not burdensome" (1 John 5:3).

"It's all too slick", someone objects. "Christ's yoke isn't *always* easy, and his burden isn't *always* light. For Christ himself insisted that the Way is a *hard* way, and the gate through which we enter upon this Way is a *narrow* gate." We can't pretend anything else. Jesus certainly insisted that the gate is narrow and the way hard. In other words, sometimes obeying God is demanding, abrasive and painful. Simply put, there are times and places and situations where obedience is difficult, onerous and arduous—excruciating even.

After World War II Corrie ten Boom, the Dutch woman who was one of the few survivors of Ravensbrueck, was shopping at a department store one day when she recognized the man a few persons ahead of her in the line-up at the cash register; he had been a guard who had abused her in that terrible camp where her sister Betsie had perished. Suddenly she was on the point of becoming unglued. Still, as a disciple of Jesus Christ she knew what she was supposed to do. Certainty about what she had to do and rage concerning this man warred within her until the certainty rose above the rage. She staggered up to the man and identified herself to him. She told him that in the name of Jesus Christ she forgave him.

Whenever she related this story subsequently someone in the audience invariably remarked how wonderful it was that the whole thing was over and done with at that moment, that she walked away from it right there, knew it was all behind her and never thought of it again. "Are you kidding?" Corrie always said, "Every morning when I get up I see that man's hideous face again, and I go to the floor all over until I can stumble back to forgiving him once more."

Parishioners often visit their pastor inasmuch as they are temptation-prone in one area of life especially. It can be any area at all. It's not that life in general is hard for them (or at least no harder for them than it is for everyone else.) It's not even that walking the Christian way in general is insuperably difficult for them. Nevertheless, in the one area of their besetting temptation the Way is exceedingly hard. We shouldn't pretend anything else. Jesus never suggested anything else.

Yet I am convinced that to "tough out" the hard spots is still to know blessing and freedom. When I was on a rigorous canoe trip in Northern Ontario recently I came upon breathtaking scenery, the glorious scenery that Tom Thomson and the Group of Seven have painted wonderfully. The scenery changed from quiet rivers to small lakes to Georgian Bay with its shoreside abandoned lumber town and the rich history one could imagine in such a place. But of course in order to lose oneself in this scenery and its beauty one had to get through the portages. Portaging, everyone knows, is never the fun that paddling is. Portaging heavy loads in dehydrating summer heat while being buzzed by black flies you don't have a hand free to swat—this is irksome. Yet it's only as we sweat through the portages persistently, as cheerfully as we can, that we can know the certain delight on the other side of them.

And therefore at the end of the day I remain convinced that obedience to our Lord Jesus Christ is *the* way to genuine freedom and profoundest blessings.

If we call Jesus "Lord" then we should obey him, especially since obeying him will alone prove that his yoke is easy, and prove as well that in shouldering *this* yoke we are living as our Father intends his children to live lest they forfeit his reward.

4

DO YOU SAY THIS OF YOUR OWN ACCORD, OR DID OTHERS SAY IT TO YOU ABOUT ME?

Pilate entered the praetorium again and called Jesus, and said to him, "Are you the King of the Jews?" Jesus answered, "Do you say this of your own accord, or did others say it to you about me?" Pilate answered, "Am I a Jew? Your own nation and the chief priests have handed you over to me; what have you done?" Jesus answered, "My kingship is not of this world; if my kingship were of this world, my servants would fight, that I might not be handed over to the Jews; but my kingship is not from the world." Pilate said to him, "So you are a king?" Jesus answered, "You say that I am a king. For this I was born, and for this I have come into the world, to bear witness to the truth. Every one who is of the truth hears my voice." Pilate said to him, "What is truth?" After he had said this, he went out to the Jews again, and told them, "I find no crime in him."

—John 18:33-38

Gossip and hearsay aren't the same. Gossip is unfounded whispering, unfounded whispering that tarnishes someone else's name, weakens her reputation, even destroys her. Gossip is both untrue and harmful.

Hearsay, on the other hand, isn't necessarily untrue or harmful. In fact, hearsay is often true and helpful. Hearsay, after all, is how we acquire most of our knowledge about the world. We have been told on good account that the sun is 90-plus million miles from the earth. But we have never measured or calculated the distance of the sun from the earth. We have taken someone else's word for it. I heard it said, and I believed it.

As it is with our knowledge of science, so it is with our knowledge of history. Napoleon besieged Moscow in 1812, sacrificing thousands of French soldiers in a dreadful military blunder. Did it actually happen? We have to take someone else's word for it. Plainly what we affirm is hearsay. And just as plainly there's nothing wrong with accepting such hearsay.

Yet there remains a setting where hearsay isn't accepted at all: a courtroom. No courtroom judge puts any stock in the testimony of someone who says, "I never actually saw Mrs. Brown shoot her husband, but when I was at the grocery store, or maybe it was the barber shop, I heard it said that she shot him." Hearsay isn't acceptable when testimony has to be rendered in a court of law.

* * * * *

Already it's evident where hearsay is acceptable and where not. It's acceptable with respect to acquiring information; but it isn't acceptable with respect to testimony concerning persons. As we move from information about things to acquaintance with persons hearsay has no place. If you were to ask me what it is to love a woman and be loved by a woman, my answer might sound somewhat self-conscious and rather awkward. Still, I profoundly know, unshakeably know, in my heart what it is to love and be loved by a woman. However awkwardly I might convey this to you, neither of us would be helped by consulting a textbook on gynaecology. Information of any kind, however sophisticated, is never a substitute for intimate acquaintance with a person.

Words always become less adequate, less helpful, as we move deeper and deeper into what is profoundly human. In fact words can never finally do justice to human intimacy. There's a level of experience that others can apprehend only if they come to share the experience themselves. They will never apprehend the experience by having it described in words.

Think of Hannah's anguish over her childlessness. Hannah is heartsick and can't eat. Her husband, Elkanah, helpless here himself, asks her, "Why do you weep? Am I not more to you than ten sons?" Elkanah simply hasn't apprehended the horror gripping Hannah's heart. How could any man understand what it is for a woman to be barren?

After my mother had been a widow for several years I came upon C. S. Lewis' fine book, *A Grief Observed*. He wrote the book following the death of his wife. The book begins very powerfully: "No one ever told me that grief was so much like being mildly concussed or being mildly drunk...." I decided to give it to my mother. A few weeks later she thanked me for the book. "It's very good," she remarked, and then added, "But what would you know about it?" Her point was valid. I have never lost the one human being who is *the* earthly comfort and consolation of my life; I have never lost the one human being to whom I've been grafted, the loss of whom, therefore, is nothing less than dismemberment.

It's firsthand acquaintance with the Word of the Lord that makes the prophet a *prophet*. The prophet is the immediate recipient of that unmistakable address from the mouth of the living God. The prophet speaks only because someone has first spoken to him. Once God has spoken to him, however, the prophet *must* speak himself. "The Word of the Lord is a fire in my mouth," cries Jeremiah, "If I don't open my mouth and let it out I'll be scorched." The false prophet, on the other hand, is under no such compulsion just because the false prophet has no firsthand acquaintance. The false prophet merely babbles and blabbers.

I'm convinced that the spiritually sensitive among us can distinguish between the preacher who speaks because he's first been spoken to and the preacher who simply blathers Sunday by Sunday. Discerning people aren't fooled.

* * * * *

The matter of discernment surfaced with Pilate. Some religious leaders hauled Jesus before Pilate and said, "This man's an evildoer. Fix him." These leaders were hostile to Jesus while Pilate was not. On the other hand, Pilate could enact the death sentence while they could not; hence their request that Pilate "fix" Jesus. Pilate had on his hands someone whom he didn't dislike, yet also someone around whom an uprising might develop. Social turbulence would tell Pilate's superiors that he couldn't do his job; his career would be at risk. Wearily Pilate asks Jesus, "*Are* you king of the Jews?" And as Jesus does characteristically when he's asked a question, he doesn't answer. Instead he asks his own question: "Am *I* king of the Jews? Do you say this of your own accord, or did others say it to you about me?" In other words, "Do you have

45

firsthand acquaintance with me, with the truth that I am, or are you merely parroting hearsay?"

"Am I a Jew?" Pilate retorts; "How on earth do you expect me to know?"

"My kingdom isn't of this world," Jesus comes back.

"Ah, so you *are* a king," says Pilate.

"Do you say this of your own accord or did others say it to you about me? You say that I am king," continues Jesus; "...I have come to bear witness to the truth." Then, in a voice steeped in weariness and frustration and vexation and cynicism Pilate mutters, "What is truth, anyway?"

"Truth," in John's gospel, always the force of "reality." "What is real, anyway?" This is what Pilate is asking, and is asking just because he doesn't know.

Pilate doesn't know who Jesus Christ is. He has heard lots *said about* our Lord, but he has had no firsthand acquaintance with our Lord, born of keeping company with him. Oddly, such firsthand acquaintance with Jesus is the common possession of apostles whose names the world will never forget as well as of countless ordinary Christians whose names the world has never remembered; and such firsthand acquaintance with Jesus is utterly foreign to Pilate. Because it's foreign to Pilate, cruel compromise comes easy to him. So what if Jesus has to be sacrificed to keep religious leaders happy, an unruly crowd at bay, and Pilate's own career intact. What's one more ragged Jewish victim of Imperial Rome's political expedience?

Let's be fair to Pilate. Who Jesus Christ is also escapes the religious leaders. They insist he's an "enemy of the people." It isn't true. Jesus isn't an enemy of Israel; he's the fulfilment of Israel. The religious leaders haven't perceived this. Meanwhile one question continues to reverberate: "Do you say this (who or what I am) of your own accord, or did others say it to you about me?" In other words, "Do you have firsthand acquaintance with me, or are you merely repeating hearsay?"

The question that reverberated then reverberates still. It has to be dealt with today. "Do you sing hymns and repeat confessions of faith and say 'Amen' to the prayers of your own accord, or did others say it to you about me?" "Do your hymns and prayers and creeds and worship-services and church meetings; does all of this come from your intimate acquaintance with me or are you merely repeating hearsay that you picked up from who knows where?" The question is still asked, and still it must be answered.

* * * * *

As we move away from picking up mere hearsay about Jesus to our own intimate acquaintance with him, what *difference* is it going to make to us?

First of all it will give us *assurance* of our faith in Jesus Christ, assurance of his hold on us, assurance that we are his younger brothers and sisters and citizens of his Father's kingdom. It will give us assurance that we are being used of God now and are destined to see our Lord face-to-face. Our Christian foreparents spoke much of assurance. Calvin said starkly, "Where there is no assurance of faith there is no faith at all." I think his assertion was too strong. Wesley said (at least at one point), "Assurance is the privilege of every believer." I think his assertion was too weak. In scripture it is simply taken for granted that those who genuinely know Jesus and love him also know that they know, know that they are loved of their Lord and are bound to him. The first epistle of John, for instance, is one of the shortest books in scripture (five brief chapters), yet the confident, firm, emphatic "We know" is found fifteen times in it. "We know that we have passed from death to life; we know that God abides in us."

To be sure there's always the "we know" of the know-it-all: insuffer-able pomposity. There's also the "we know" of prejudice: "We just know that immigrants are corrupt and they take away 'our' jobs." There's even the "we know" of outright ignorance where nothing is known. Nevertheless, when all this is taken into account we are left with the conviction, spirit and word of the apostle John and countless Christians after him: "He who believes in the Son of God has the testimony in himself."

Decades ago when I was studying for the ministry we had to preach to our seminary classmates in our homiletics courses. One of my classmates, entirely unawares, preached a sermon in which he said many times over, no doubt out of habit, "I suppose...." When he had finished, the homiletics instructor, an older Church of Scotland minister whose faith was as deep as a well, stared at the student and said, "You suppose? You *suppose*? Young man, when you mount the pulpit steps either you *know* or you don't say anything. No one is going to have her faith strengthened by a preacher who merely supposes."

"He who believes in the Son of God has the testimony in himself." Faith born of intimate acquaintance with our Lord brings with it the assurance that confirms us every day in the truth and reality of the Lord to whom our faith has bound us.

In the second place, as we move from hearsay to acquaintance we shall magnify the credibility of the gospel itself. We shall render more believable *for others* the fact that Jesus Christ *is* truth and life and way; that there's forgiveness and freedom for any repentant person at all; there's comfort and strength and healing and a constantly renewed 'new beginning' for anyone who may know little or much about Jesus but above all clings to him and wants only to cling more closely. As we move from hearsay to acquaintance *we* shall be the magnifying glass that causes the truth and substance of the gospel to loom so large as to be both unmistakable and unavoidable. Possessed *by* the gospel, we shall always be the most effective advertisement *for* the gospel. As we radiate not an arrogant cocksureness but rather the simple assurance of those who *know* that living in the company of Jesus Christ is better than any alternative; as we radiate this, discipleship will become ever more attractive to people whose life-needs, like ours, cry out for the gospel yet who haven't found the Christian way attractive to date.

Lastly, as we move from hearsay about our Lord to acquaintance with him we shall see him whole. There's always a tendency to see Jesus Christ fragmented, bits and pieces of him here and there; a saying, a parable or two, a pronouncement on this or that. People latch onto a piece of him, a partial truth, one aspect of him, and then assume that this one piece or aspect or partial truth is all there is.

For instance, people hear what he said about the danger of riches (no doubt he said it and meant it) and then they assume that he supports any ill-conceived program of social disruption resulting in social dismantling. Or they hear what he said about rising early to pray and seeking his Father's face in private, only to think he supports a pietistic escapism that turns its back on the human distress around us, distress that we can address and should. Or they see him elevate women (unquestionably he did) and then tell us that the gospel supports every last plank in the shrillest feminist platform, even where aspects of that platform deny the gospel.

The only way we avoid reducing our Lord to one aspect of him; which is to say, the only way we avoid shredding him grotesquely is to encounter and cherish all of him. This isn't difficult. Genuinely to meet someone anywhere in life is always to meet that person in her totality. The whole Master is what God has given us. Then why should we settle for less? What's more, since the whole Master has been given to us, we must have him whole or we shan't have him at all. It's as we move from hearsay about him to acquaintance with him that we embrace the whole of him who has been given to us, only to learn that he has always longed to possess us wholly.

"Do you say this on your own, of your own accord, or did others say it to you about me?" Jesus put this question to Pilate. Pilate fumbled and stumbled and faltered, for he knew what he was meant to say he couldn't say truthfully, and what he could say truthfully he wasn't meant to say.

The same question is put to us. "Do you have firsthand, intimate acquaintance with me, or are you merely mouthing whatever you've absorbed unknowingly from your environment?" Our Lord expects us to reply, "Of our own, on our own accord;" and having rendered this reply once, to render it again and again as we seize him afresh, faith is renewed, and we follow him forever.

49

5

DO YOU THINK THAT
I HAVE COME TO GIVE
PEACE ON EARTH?

*"I came to cast fire upon the earth; and would that it were
already kindled! I have a baptism to be baptized with; and
how I am constrained until it is accomplished! Do you think
that I have come to give peace on earth? No, I tell you, but
rather division; for henceforth in one house there will be five
divided, three against two and two against three; they will
be divided, father against son and son against father, mother
against daughter and daughter against her mother, mother-in-
law against her daughter-in-law and daughter-in-law against
her mother-in-law."*

—Luke 12:49-53

"War is hell", said General Sherman, the Northern military leader who campaigned throughout the South, perpetrating whatever devastation was deemed necessary for the preservation of the union. Sherman was right. The material losses are staggering. Sherman set fire to the city of Atlanta, Georgia, and burnt it to the ground; his "scorched earth" policy in rural areas hastened the termination of the war as southern civilians found themselves with little to eat.

As bad as the material losses in war are, however, the human destruction is worse. The physical pain and dismemberment and disability remain incomprehensible. Beyond the physical distresses are the psychiatric horrors. We hear less about the psychiatric horrors of war, if only because they are less visible to the public. For all that, however, they are no less nightmarish. In World War II psychiatric breakdown was the single largest reason for honourable discharge from the armed forces. Any combatant's chances of psychiatric collapse (from the American Civil War right up to Israel's invasion of Lebanon in 1982) are three times greater than his likelihood of being killed. When the U.S. army landed in Sicily in the 1940s there were platoons where the psychiatric breakdown was 100%. Military psychiatrists have found that the only combatant who doesn't collapse, regardless of how long he is under fire, is the full-blown psychopath.

Then what does Jesus have in mind when he says, "Do you think that I've come to bring peace to the earth? I haven't come to bring peace, but a sword, division"? It's all the more startling in view of the fact that the apostles speak of our Lord as the prince of peace. The announcement made to the shepherds at his birth was "peace on earth." And then a few years later he is telling us that he *hasn't* come to bring peace on earth? Then what does he mean when he insists that he's come to bring strife?

* * * * *

We begin to understand our Lord as we remember that he stood in the line of Israel's prophets. Certainly the prophets longed for *shalom*, God's definitive peace, nothing less than the entire creation healed. Yet just as surely the prophets knew that there can never be peace without justice. Any attempt at promoting peace without doing justice is fraudulent.

For years we engaged in polite conversations that discussed the situation in South Africa. "Why can't black people and white people simply get along together? Why can't they live at peace?" But there can be no real peace without justice. Peter Botha, the former prime minister, maintained that his people, white people, would never dismantle apartheid willingly. Apartheid began to crumble only when the economic gun was held to the head of white South Africa. Yet holding a gun of any sort to someone's head is scarcely evidence of peace.

A common misunderstanding always lurking in the church is that Jesus is always and everywhere the great "smoother-over." Whenever he found antagonistic people or tense situations he acted as a neutral broker and smoothed things over. The written gospels, however, paint a very different picture. According to them, wherever Jesus went there was a disruption.

Jesus comes upon some orthodox folk who care more for their religious reputations and their supposed religious superiority than they will ever care for personal integrity and transparency before God. To them Jesus says, "You people go halfway around the world to lasso one convert, and when you finally get him you make him twice as much a child of hell as you are yourselves." Disruption. Next day Jesus comes upon some people who think they have preferential status before God just because they are Israelites. "There were many widows in Israel in the days when Jezebel, a wicked woman, was seeking the prophet Elijah in order to kill him", says Jesus. "But who took Elijah, Israel's greatest prophet, into her home and provided sanctuary for him at terrible risk to herself? A widow from a nation you Israelites pronounce 'godless.'" Another disruption.

* * * * *

The truth is, wherever Jesus went there *was* conflict. Yet Jesus never caused trouble for the sake of causing trouble. He didn't have a personality disorder that relished upheaval. He caused a disruption only in order that his hearers might finally hear and heed and do the truth of God, therein finding the profoundest peace of God. Whenever our Lord caused pain he did so only in order that the people whom he plunged into greater pain might submit themselves to the great physician himself. Whenever God's truth is held up in a world of falsehood there's going to be disruption. There has to be disruption if the *shalom* of God is going to appear.

Surely this isn't difficult to understand. We know that the person whose medical condition is making her uncomfortable must undergo treatment that will make her even more uncomfortable—at least for a while—if she's to get better. It's the same with psychotherapy. If we are distressed by the emotional distortions that haunt us, we have to own the distortions with their attendant pain, and find ourselves feeling worse—at least for a while—before we find relief.

* * * * *

We should make no mistake. Jesus insists we owe him our ultimate love and loyalty. He, his word, his kingdom, his way, and his truth: this must take first place in our lives. As we honour our Lord's pre-eminent claim upon our life, love, and loyalty, we must admit that other loves and loyalties are going to have to take second place. Some of them won't like this. Jesus warns us of this and leaves us with a reminder so stark we can't forget it: "Whoever loves father or mother more than me; whoever loves son or daughter more than me isn't worthy of me." Our own family members may resent him and us when they see that they don't have first claim on us and aren't going to have.

When Father Damien announced that he was leaving his home in Belgium to work with lepers on the island of Molokai, a dot in middle of the Pacific Ocean, we can't imagine that his mother leapt for joy. Likely she reminded him tartly that he should be a little more considerate of her widowhood. After all, if he wanted to be a priest he could be a priest just as readily in Belgium as he could in the Hawaiian Islands, couldn't he? Furthermore, since sinners are sinners, why bother abandoning her and endangering himself to work with *leper*-sinners? If he wanted to work with despised people, outcasts, there was certainly no shortage of such people in Europe. What's more, why not let a priest who was already leprosy-plagued minister to the men on Molokai? Yet the voice of Jesus reverberated in Damien's heart: "He who loves father or mother more than me isn't worthy of me. A man's foes will be those of his own household. Whoever doesn't take up his cross and *obey* me can't be my disciple." Damien knew he had to go to Molokai. And if some members of his family couldn't understand why and faulted him for going, that wasn't his problem.

My own mother and father knew that parents can get in the way of that discipleship to which God has called their son or daughter; they can unwittingly deflect their child's first love and loyalty away from Jesus Christ. Parents have plans for their children, grand plans more often than not. Parents can wish for their child a life of greater ease, greater comfort, greater remuneration, less renunciation than God ordains for their child in view of the service to which God is calling their child. Knowing this, my parents made a public declaration, concerning me, in a service of public worship when I was only six weeks old. They declared that as far as they were able they would never deflect me from any obedience and service to Jesus Christ and to his kingdom that my vocation might entail. Once in a while I read over the words that were read aloud to my parents and to which my parents replied, "We promise." Here they are. "You must be willing that Victor Allan should spend all his life for God wherever God should choose to send him, and not withhold him at any time from such *hardship, suffering, want or sacrifice* as true devotion to the service of Christ may entail." My parents knew that if they nurtured me to be a disciple of Jesus Christ; that is, if they nurtured me to give *him* my ultimate love and loyalty yet subtly, even unknowingly, wanted my final allegiance to be to them and their plans for me, then they would find that Jesus hadn't brought peace to the Shepherd household but rather a sword.

We shouldn't assume that our Lord can cause a disruption only in families; he causes disruptions in any social grouping: friends, colleagues, club mates, workmates. One of my friends, a schoolteacher, was admitted to the principal-track. The board of education sent him, together with all the candidates, on a principal's summer course in a city 150 kilometres away from the precincts of the Board of Education they all served. Everyone was now guaranteed relative anonymity. Virtually everyone on the course was married; virtually no one behaved this way. There were pairings-off and six-week liaisons and experiments in group-this and group-that, as well as visits to a nightclub whose chief entertainment was table dancers. My friend excused himself from all of this as gently and quietly as he could. He tried extra-hard not to point the finger at anyone. Nastily he was queried as to why he wasn't participating. He said simply that what he was asked to do contradicted his Christian profession; which profession, he added, he wasn't expecting anyone else to make. Immediately the other principal-trainees on the course fell on him. He was told he was a self-righteous prig, a do-gooder, a "brown-noser." It was suggested he was trying to accumulate merit points that he could cash in for Board of Education promotion. He was resented inasmuch as others felt he now had information on them that was scarcely going to improve their reputations or enhance their marriages. He was threatened that he had better be wise enough to know when to keep his mouth shut. The mood on the summer course had become sheer hostility. Jesus Christ had brought a sword. And the discomfort my friend had to endure for the remainder of the course was the cross he had to take up.

* * * * *

Yet we mustn't think that discipleship is unrelieved drudgery. The opposite is the case. Jesus promised he would reward—hugely—anyone who cherished him and stood with him in all circumstances at whatever cost. He promised that such people were going to "find" their life. Even crossbearing, a necessary part of intimacy with Jesus, would become not a living death (as so many expect) but the infusion that makes life *life.*

Our Lord keeps his promises. Whoever follows him and stands with him and endures whatever unpopularity or abuse all of this might entail; *this* person he will hold up and honour and bless; *this* person he will never abandon or let down or betray.

We hear a great deal today about people who decide it's time they "found" themselves. They haven't found themselves to this point, they are convinced, and time is slipping away on them. Usually they assume that the root to finding themselves is to veer suddenly in a startlingly new direction. Too often they veer impulsively into an ill-considered career change or spouse change. They do something quixotic, bizarre, perchance something illegal with its attendant thrill. They may do something that they think will prove unusually titillating. At the end of it all they are jaded, and are no closer to finding themselves.

The words of our Lord's piercing question—"Do you think that I have come to bring peace to the earth?"—are recorded in Luke's gospel. In Matthew's gospel Jesus follows this question with a ringing declaration concerning losing one's life and finding it. There he insists that there's only one way we are ever going to find ourselves: *we have to forget ourselves.* Yet we are to forget ourselves not in an attitude of self-belittlement or self-contempt; we are to "forget" ourselves only because we have become preoccupied with him and his kingdom and all we must be about. For it's now plain to us that his kingdom has been superimposed on the kingdoms of his world, and his kingdom, startlingly vivid, has relativized everything we regarded as unarguable up to this point.

If we are sceptical of this, if it sounds too slick for us, then we should immerse ourselves in Christian biography. (Reading the biographies of Christ's people remains my favourite form of leisure activity; and more than "leisure", since I have found no comparable spiritual tonic.) As we steep ourselves in Christian biography we find that it becomes a means of grace for us, a vehicle that carries us away from ourselves and into the realm and service of God. We find ourselves losing ourselves for the sake of the kingdom of God, only to discover that in "losing" ourselves we are never lost to God. Instead, we know, with a conviction deeper than the sceptic's scoffing, that we've been found of God and are cherished by him and will be satisfied in him for as long as breath remains in us. In short, we have verified our Lord's promise: "Whoever keeps her life will lose it, and whoever loses her life for my sake will find it."

Jesus came not to bring peace, he tells us, but a sword, division, strife, trouble and turbulence. He means that the disruption he causes is surgery necessary to re-set what's fractured, put right what's dislocated, cleanse what's infected. In short, the pain he causes is curative in that it's the beginning of the *shalom* of God. Even though he brings a sword; even *as* he brings a sword and causes division, he is and remains first and finally the reconciler, the bringer of peace, for he *is* the prince of peace, and was given us to bring peace to the earth.

To be possessed of this certainty is to abandon ourselves to him, therein to discover that we have found ourselves—and all of this inasmuch as we've been found of him.

6

WHO TOUCHED ME?

*And a woman who had had a flow of blood for twelve years
and could not be healed by any one, came up behind him, and
touched the fringe of his garment; and immediately her flow
of blood ceased. And Jesus said, "Who was it that touched
me?" When all denied it, Peter said, "Master, the multitudes
surround you and press upon you!" But Jesus said, "Some one
touched me; for I perceive that power has gone forth from
me."And when the woman saw that she was not hidden, she
came trembling, and falling down before him declared in
the presence of all the people why she had touched him, and
how she had been immediately healed. And he said to her,
"Daughter, your faith has made you well; go in peace."*

—Luke 8:43-48

"To see and be seen," said my grade nine geography teacher; "This is why people go to tourist beaches, to ski resorts, and to church; to see and be seen." Perhaps he was right decades ago. Perhaps there was a day when some people came to church for this reason. They wanted to see; i.e., catch up on gossip. They wanted to be seen; i.e., preserve their standing in the community, even be able to do business on Monday. But we live in a different era now. Today no one comes to church for this reason.

Then why do people come to church? Curiosity might bring a few, but if curiosity brought them it would never keep them, because there isn't much in church for curiosity seekers. We don't traffic in oddities or secrets or spookiness. What the church traffics in happens to be simple, transparent, and highly repetitive. We sing hymns that congregations have sung for centuries; we read from a book that a child can read; we listen to an address that uses illustrations everywhere lest people go home mystified. I'm convinced that people come to church today largely for the same reason that the woman in our text stood, with scores of others, in a crowd. The reason, Luke tells us, was that she had heard reports about Jesus.

Reports about Jesus abounded in the days of his earthly ministry. We are told that the common people heard him gladly and turned out in droves at the same time that religious leaders suspected him and conspired behind closed doors. One report about Jesus was that he was compassionate; it's no wonder people kept bringing their sick and disturbed to him. And yet as compassionate as he was, people wouldn't have kept bringing their sick and disturbed to him unless he was more than compassionate; he had to be helpful as well, effective. People came to him, lingered with him, and then bound themselves to him for one reason: in his company they became different; life became different; the world became different; *everything* became different.

People come to church today for the same reason. They have heard reports about Jesus. They have heard that he receives and helps those whom life has jarred and jolted, even wounded and warped.

People are shaken up when they are surprised to discover they weren't able to anticipate how they reacted to blows and irruptions and disruptions. To be sure, all of us try to anticipate how we are going to react as we imagine a blow or an upheaval befalling us. When the catastrophe, or merely an irruption, does happen, however, we discover that what we were able to anticipate in our heads we weren't able to anticipate in our hearts. How we reacted had virtually nothing to do with how we had thought we were going to react. And now we fear irruptions in life as we didn't fear them before.

The younger person, even the younger adult, unconsciously thinks himself to be invulnerable. If you sat him down and queried him about life's vulnerabilities, he'd say, "Of course I'm aware that accident, disease, disaster can overtake anyone at any time. Do you think I'm naïve or stupid?" Still, what he admits with his conscious, reflective mind he hasn't yet admitted with his unconscious mind. And it's the unconscious mind that has such telling effect in everyone's life. Then one day something befalls him that drives home at *all* levels of his mind something he'd always admitted with his head but never with his heart: life is fragile; life is precarious; life is brief; life is subject to vulnerabilities that can never be rendered invulnerable.

Most of us spend years without reflecting critically on the assumption (actually it's an illusion) that we are in control. We are in control of ourselves (of course); not only of ourselves but also of our family, of our colleagues, of a significant corner of our world. Then one day events force us to admit—finally—that while the sphere of our influence may be great, the sphere of our control is minuscule. And now we aren't even sure we're in control of ourselves.

For years we remain untouched by grief in that we have suffered no overwhelming loss, and untouched by guilt if only because we think ourselves superior to everyone else. Then piercing loss fuels grief, and a realistic awareness that others find our sin repugnant adds guilt to grief.

For years we listen to other people complain that they find life meaningless; we quietly pride ourselves on the fact that we don't find it meaningless if only because we're too busy to ponder the significance of everything that fills up and overflows our life. One day, however, we realize that our problem isn't life's meaninglessness; our problem is life's meanings: there are so many of them, so many that are incompatible; and in any case there's no single, true meaning, trustworthy meaning, eternal meaning. Our problem, we see, isn't meaninglessness; our problem, rather, is a welter of contradictory meanings that finds us threatened with fragmentation.

* * * * *

At this point we're like the woman in our text: "If I but touch the fringe of his clothes, I shall be made well; just the fringe." In first century Palestine men wore their talith, their prayer shawl, as an undershirt. The prayer shawl therefore remained hidden under their workday clothing, except for the tassels at the four corners of the prayer shawl; these hung down below their workday shirt. The needy woman felt that by grasping these she was making contact with *him*, and this would be sufficient. It would be enough *merely* to make contact. There'd be no need to spout elaborate introductions or offer effusive explanations. Besides, she was a woman and he was a man; men and women didn't converse in public. She was suffering from an ailment that would make others in the community shrink from her. It would be better to say nothing, act boldly, and see what happens next. All she wanted to do was *make contact.* What's more, the four tassels symbolized the truth that the Word of God reaches to the four corners of the earth. If it really reaches to the four outermost corners of the earth, she thought, perhaps it reaches to my tiny corner of the earth, to *me.*

Let's not deceive ourselves. People at their profoundest come to church because they have heard reports concerning Jesus Christ, and they've been told that the building labelled "church" and the institution "church" have something to do with him and may even help them make contact with him. People at their profoundest come to church because they think that their chances of meeting him and finding help are better there.

I'm convinced it's no different with us who have been coming to church for a long time and will continue to come. To be sure, there is much here that appears to have little to do with reaching out to touch our Lord: shingling the roof, gassing the furnace, paying the electricity bill. The truth is, however, all of these matters have everything to do with making contact with him. It's for this purpose only that we shingle the roof and gas the furnace and pay for electricity.

The woman in our text again: what did she think that merely touching our Lord was going to do for her? Was there an element, or more than an element, of superstition in what she did? There may have been. If there was, I'm sure our Lord would have corrected it eventually; he wouldn't have allowed her to go on touching him as if she were pressing a button that gave her a charge. He wouldn't have allowed her to keep pawing him mechanically as though voodoo-like superstition could ever substitute for spiritual maturity. Over and over in the written gospels Jesus receives those who come to him with whatever defective understanding, and then moves them beyond a misunderstanding of him that is so woefully immature as to be spiritually threatening. When the mother of James and John wanted positions of privilege for her two sons Jesus told her she was asking the wrong question; she should have been asking if her two sons were resilient enough to endure the long-term rigours of disciple-ship without quitting. Of course he would expect an apprehension of him deeper than feeling the fringes of his prayer shawl. He would have corrected the woman *eventually*; but he didn't correct her instantly.

For our Lord knows something we must never forget: before we can begin to mature we have to be born. Before we step ahead maturely in the Christian life, we have to take a first step. And the difference between no step and first step is a quantum leap. In short, there are two dangers we must avoid. One danger is expecting ourselves and others to exhibit exemplary spiritual maturity without first having touched our Lord. When this happens we expect people to swim confidently in the waters of Christian wisdom and devotional richness and spiritual discernment and self-renouncing service when in fact they can't swim at all. They splash around for a while repeating formulas they don't understand and pursuing a pathway they find pointless until one day they give up the whole thing, and we never see them in church again. The other danger is making contact, all right, and then fixating ourselves at an infantile level of Christian understanding and venture, content to make contact, plainly enough, but never moving on to that maturity in Christ which Paul says is ultimately the goal of Christian ministry.

* * * * *

The woman touches Jesus. "Who touched me?" he says. "Someone has touched me. Who is it?" The disciples remind him that the crowd resembles the subway train at rush hour: people are squeezed together so tightly that everyone is touching a dozen others. Who has touched him? Who hasn't touched him? The question is silly.

Except that it isn't. "Some *one* person has touched me," Jesus insists. "Within this crowd there is some one *person* who has moved from observing me and assessing me to contacting me. Who is it?"

Today our society seems on the point of forgetting what richness the gospel has brought the society in terms of our understanding of the person, and how quickly that gospel-inspired leaven can depart the society.

Think of the hideousness that Marxism fostered. In the Marxist set-up the individual person counts for nothing. The collective counts for everything. The individual has no rights at all. The individual has merit only because of the individual's place in the collective. Any exploitation of the individual, however cruel or even deadly, is legitimate if it serves the greater good (so-called) of the collective. We're all aware of the forced labour camps in Siberia and the Gulag system and Stalin's systematic starvation of twelve million people in the Ukraine and the 30 to 60 million people that the secret police took down—not to mention the 90 million that Mao Tse Tung liquidated in "The People's Revolution" of communist China.

Think of a spectacle seen every day in India. I saw it myself. Someone collapses on the street, manifestly ill. People step around her or step over her but don't stop to help her. After all, fate, the gods, have willed that she be stricken at this moment, fall in this position, and remain there. To lend assistance is to defy what the gods have willed and therein to court the gods' displeasure. Therefore wise people leave the victim alone. On my first day in India I came upon a dog that had been dead for several days. Maggots were crawling in and out of the carcase. It stank unimaginably. But no one had buried the carcase. After all, the gods had appointed the dog to die in that position on that day. To remove the remains would court retaliation on the part of the deities.

And then I think of a parishioner in my Mississauga congregation who suffered a major heart attack. He was sustained by the most up-to-date medical wizardry, was given a heart transplant, and underwent many more surgeries until his chest and abdomen resembled a quilt. The cost of all this, borne by the taxpayer, seemed to be approaching the national debt. While he was mending from the heart transplant he had to have his gall bladder removed. Only seven years later he died anyway. Yet no one ever said of him, "He isn't worth it. People die of heart trouble every day. What's so special about him? Besides, he's costing too much. Let him go." No one even whispered this.

How long do we think such a commitment to the needy individual whose treatment isn't "cost-effective" will continue once our society has become thoroughly secularized and the indirect illumination of the gospel has disappeared entirely?

It's been pointed out several times over that in a Marxist collectivity the individual is worthless. The reason the individual is worthless here is that the individual isn't a person; the individual is merely a cog in a giant machine, and any cog can replace any other cog.

Strictly speaking, ancient Greek philosophy knew of the individual; it did not, however, know of the person. The notion of the *person* is the church's gift to the world. The difference is this: the individual is an individual in herself, but a person is always person-in-relation. So far as the individual is concerned, to exist is to be; but so far as the person is concerned, to exist is to be-in-relation. To exist as a person is never the same as existing as an individual. Ancient Greek philosophy spoke of the individual but never of the person. The church knew the difference and insisted that every last human being is a person.

Admittedly, there are some human beings whose lives are wretched. They appear to be friendless. They appear to be isolated. They appear to be abandoned, forsaken. But in fact there is no human being anywhere, at any time, who is ultimately abandoned and finally forsaken, just because there is no human being whom God doesn't cherish.

We must be sure we see the woman in our story in proper context. She reached out to touch our Lord—intentionally, wilfully, deliberately seeking help. Others didn't. Then did they lack all relation to Jesus Christ? Do such people still? The truth is, in his death our Lord embraced every last human being without exception, without qualification, without reservation, without hesitation. Because of his embrace every human being is a person with respect to him. Remember, to exist is to be-in-relation. The arms of the crucified ensure not only that individuals are individuals rather than faceless cogs in a cosmic machine; the arms of the crucified ensure that no one is finally forsaken, no one ultimately abandoned, no one bereft of that "other" who guarantees that all individuals are, more profoundly still, persons.

The church's gift to the world here is breathtaking, and nowadays most of the world doesn't know by whom the gift was given. What will be the shape, the texture, of our society if, or when, the indirect illumination of the gospel recedes and the society is left not even with the wisdom that ancient Greek philosophy could muster, but merely with the new barbarism that looms around us?

I remain convinced that the indirect illumination still lighting our society might remain if the church continues to hold up the direct lighting of the gospel. Only the gospel insists that any one person matters inestimably to God just because only the gospel insists—just because all human beings exist in relation to Jesus Christ—that all persons are *persons*.

* * * * *

Sunday after Sunday we are found at worship for many different reasons. One reason, surely, is that we want to make contact with our Lord again. Centuries ago a needy woman, a courageous woman, reached out and grabbed the tassels of his prayer shawl, believing thereby she would find in him what she needed most.

"Who has touched me?" She had. She mattered supremely to him; but ultimately no more than all of us matter to him, for he has first touched us all with outstretched arms, thereby rendering us persons whose worth, importance and gifts are beyond price.

We in the church know this. We want to remind the wider society of this truth lest our society forget it and thereby imperil everyone.

7

WHAT'S YOUR NAME?

They came to the other side of the sea, to the country of the Ger'asenes. And when he had come out of the boat, there met him out of the tombs a man with an unclean spirit, who lived among the tombs; and no one could bind him any more, even with a chain; for he had often been bound with fetters and chains, but the chains he wrenched apart, and the fetters he broke in pieces; and no one had the strength to subdue him. Night and day among the tombs and on the mountains he was always crying out, and bruising himself with stones. And when he saw Jesus from afar, he ran and worshiped him; and crying out with a loud voice, he said, "What have you to do with me, Jesus, Son of the Most High God? I adjure you by God, do not torment me." For he had said to him, "Come out of the man, you unclean spirit!" And Jesus asked him, "What is your name?" He replied, "My name is Legion; for we are many."

—Mark 5:19

"What's your name?" Jesus asked a man on one occasion. Our Lord didn't mean what the office-worker means when she's filling out forms and asks us, "Name, address, telephone number?" If we said, "My name is Bill Smith," it would tell her no more about us than if we had said, "My name is Sam Jones." Names today tell us nothing at all about the person whom the name names. "Victor Shepherd": "Victor" is Latin for conqueror. I'm no conqueror. "Shepherd" is English for sheep-herder. I've nothing but urban blood in my veins.

When Jesus came upon a deranged man, however, and asked, "What's your name?", he was asking the man to tell him something about himself, *everything* about himself, who he most profoundly was. In the ancient world "name" meant four things: personal presence, character, power, and deserved reputation.

"What's your name?" Jesus asks every one of us today. He won't be satisfied with "My name is Samantha." He already knows that. Instead he's asking, "Samantha, when you speak and act, are you present in person, or are what you say and what you do hollow, a smokescreen meant to cloak the truth that you merely pretend to be present, attentive, engaged when you can't be bothered with people you deem inferior? Are you really available to the people you meet? Are you really accessible? Or do you smile as if you were personally present when all the while your head and your heart are anywhere but with the people in front of you?"

He's asking even more: "What's your character? Are you honest or corrupt? patient or irascible? kind or vindictive? forgiving or vengeful?"

He's also asking about power: "Are you influential or ineffective? Do you foster reconciliation or alienation? Do you spread joy or misery?"

And then in the fourth place he's asking about the reputation we deserve just because we have acted in public and never disguise ourselves as thoroughly as we think we do—if we disguise ourselves at all.

* * * * *

Centuries ago Jesus came upon a fellow who lived in the cemetery, ran about naked, and mutilated himself. No one was able to subdue him. "What's your name?" our Lord asked him. "I don't know" the fellow replied; *"How do you expect me to tell you my one name when my names are legion, there being so many of us?* What's my name? *Which one would you like to hear?* What's my character? *Which of my many 'selves' are you talking about?"* Plainly the man doesn't know who he is. He can't tell anyone anything about an identity underneath his frenzy. A legion, we should note, was a Roman military unit consisting of 4000 to 6000 men. The man feels he's all of them at once.

We think he's unlike us because he appears deranged; we take refuge in the fact that at least we aren't psychotic. Christ's question, however, addressed to us, would find us having to give the same answer. "I don't know who I am, which one I am, the reputation I am, just because there are so many of us."

How do we come to be "many?"

Think of the daily pressure to be something to one person and something else to another person and something else again to a third person. Think of how it seems we have to ease our way through tight spots in life by bending the truth here and telling just a little lie there and misrepresenting ourselves somewhere else, all in the interests of getting us or those dear to us past the social or workplace or domestic landmines and quicksands that will otherwise take us down. The truth is, of course, we are daily putting on one false face after another, always telling ourselves that underneath our exchangeable false faces there does remain a real face, our true face, our authentic identity. If no one else is aware of who we are at this point, at least we know who we are.

But it's never this simple. As we shuffle the false faces, falsity overtakes us little by little. We *tell* ourselves we haven't reduced ourselves to phoniness; we *tell* ourselves that when this sticky situation is past and dissimulation appears no longer to be needed we can revert to our real face, our true self, our proper identity. But of course life is ceaselessly fraught with sticky situations. Every day brings a host of them. Subtly we become more and more adept at interchanging false faces until we're no longer aware that any one of them is false; we're no longer aware that "false" describes not what we put forward for public consumption but who we've become ourselves; no longer aware, simply, that we have rendered ourselves phoniness incarnate.

While most of us don't have a drinking problem or a drug problem, all of us happen to be addicts. After all, we are sinners, and sin is addictive. (If sin weren't addictive we'd have long since left it behind, wouldn't we have?) Since we should admit ourselves to be addicts, we should be sobered every time we read the literature displayed by those among us who *know* they're addicts. One such item, found at meetings of Alcoholics Anonymous and Narcotics Anonymous, is the acrostic, "DENIAL", with the word spelled vertically. DENIAL: "Don't Even (k)Now I Am Lying."

Another addict slogan we should ponder: "It's not your drinking; it's your stinking thinking." Stinking thinking is thinking that the addict assumes to be the soul of reason and common sense, when anyone who knows him finds it sheer rationalization and utter stupidity.

Our name can also become "legion" through moral compromise. When we are tempted to make moral shortcuts our conscience pricks us at first and we hesitate; pricked now, we have to rationalize the compromise to pacify our conscience; conscience pacified now, we have the inner tranquility, inner permission even, to go ahead with our treachery—just this once, of course, because of extraordinary circumstances—after which we shall revert to our integrity. It seems not to occur to us that integrity which can be set aside opportunistically is no integrity at all. Very quickly the compromise becomes second nature. People wrapped up in extra-marital liaisons tell us that the first time they committed adultery they were in torment; the second time they had only a momentary twinge; the third time was as easy as falling off a wet log. Yet when someone identifies them in terms of their adultery they protest: "That isn't who or what I *really* am." It isn't? Why not?

Again, our name becomes "legion" through mindless conformity to social convention. Social conventions are necessary. Social conventions facilitate the movement of people throughout the society the way traffic lights facilitate the movement of traffic through intersections. Our society agrees to stop at red lights. But of course there's no *intrinsic* connection between red light and stopping. In the same way we "collide" less frequently socially if we all agree to abide by social conventions even though there's no intrinsic connection between arbitrary convention and the behaviour associated with it. The peril in our doing so, of course, is that the social convention comes to tell us who we are.

People customarily address me as "reverend." It's a social convention. "Reverend" means I'm revere-able, and I'm revere-able (supposedly) inasmuch as I'm extraordinarily holy. I'm also called "Doctor", Latin for "teacher." I'm extraordinarily learned. I've come to like the sound of it: "Reverend Dr." It sets me apart, doesn't it? It sets me apart from those who lack both my sanctity and my learning. "Reverend Dr.": it tells me who I am; it *makes* me who I am.

It makes me who I am, that is, until Jesus Christ looms before me and asks, "What's your name?" And when I start to say, "Reverend Dr." he butts in, "Do you think I'm fooled by social conventions? Do you think the label that you relish disguises for a minute what oozes out of your every pore?"

The sad truth is most people take as their name whatever the silent majority represents. As the silent majority shifts from this to that, picks up this and drops that, believes this now when it used to believe that then; this is what most people are. What's their name? Their name is the myriad, ill thought-out ideational clutter that forms the mental furniture and the clogged cardiac system of the silent majority. Their name is legion.

Of course there are always those who think they're smarter than most and can recognize all this. Therefore they are going to react to it: they are going to be whatever the silent majority *isn't*. Alas, they don't see that their "name" is still determined by the silent majority: reacting blindly to the silent majority, they have become the noisy minority that the silent majority has made them in any case, unbeknownst to them. Their name too is "legion."

* * * * *

The man in our gospel incident was violent. No one could restrain him. After a while no one tried. Anyone who doesn't know who she is; anyone whose identity is fragile; anyone who is forever scrambling to find an identity lest the one she doesn't really have is taken away from her in any case; any such person will behave violently.

When I was younger I used to think that people who lashed out were uncommonly nasty. Having observed people for decades, however, I see that I was wrong. Those who lash out violently and cause havoc aren't uncommonly nasty; they are commonly insecure. Their fragile, arbitrary, undefendable identity is threatened with extinction. They have to shore it up lest anyone "see through" them and discover that they are hollow inside.

When I was younger I was perplexed as to why people exploded if someone merely disagreed with them. And if they managed to stay cool when someone disagreed with them, they didn't stay cool when someone refuted them. I was perplexed that what passed for a discussion on a topic became a battle in which someone, being led to see that the point he had advanced wasn't actually sound, suddenly clung to the point regardless, enlarged it, raised his voice, reddened his face, and attempted to browbeat others into admitting he was right. The reason, of course, that it's so difficult to admit we are wrong is that our identity is tied up with a position we've adopted (regardless of the issue), and to admit we are wrong is to forfeit an identity that is so fragile in any case that it's readily toppled and soon crumbles. As thoroughly as we understand these dynamics, the next time we are threatened with loss of face and looming fragmentation we are no less likely to become violent. Anyone threatened with extinction is going to turn nasty. We shouldn't be surprised.

* * * * *

In our gospel story Jesus heals the man whose name is "legion." The townspeople find him "sitting there, clothed, and in his right mind." In the Greek text there are three pithy, pointed participles: "seated, clothed, right-minded." The three parallel participles—"seated, clothed, right-minded"—underline the fact that something definitive has occurred to the man, something conclusive, something that is as undeniable as it is unmistakable.

Seated. In Hebrew symbolism to be seated is to be in authority, to rule. Whenever a rabbi made an authoritative pronouncement he sat to speak. When Jesus delivers the Sermon on the Mount he sits to teach. Our Lord wants us to know that in the Sermon on the Mount he isn't offering an opinion; he's speaking authoritatively, sealing upon us *the* meaning of life in the kingdom of God.

Following his ascension the risen Jesus is said to be "seated at the right hand of the Father." He is seated inasmuch as his resurrection has rendered him victor and his ascension has rendered him ruler; as victorious ruler he is sovereign over the cosmos.

The man whose name had been "legion" is now found seated. He's no longer the helpless victim of whatever forces howl down upon him. He's no longer a function of everyone he's met and everything he's seen. For the first time in his life he is sovereign of himself. He is now the subject of his own existence. As subject of his own existence he's a self; *a* self; one, unitary self. Now he's simply *himself,* his own *self,* the subject of his own life. Hereafter he speaks and acts with the authority of someone who knows who he is and what he's about.

Clothed. In Hebrew symbolism to be clothed is to belong. When the prodigal son returns from the far country and comes home his father clothes him in a robe. The robe means that he belongs; he belongs to this household; he belongs in this home; he belongs with this family. He *belongs.*

In our Lord's parable of the wedding garment the guests are streaming into the reception when one fellow tries to crash the party. He isn't wearing a wedding garment. (In First Century Palestine, we must note, not merely the wedding party but the wedding guests too wore distinctive clothing.) The party-crasher is denied admission to the wedding reception. Lacking the proper clothing, he doesn't belong, and everyone knows it.

When the apostle Paul speaks of the new life that Jesus Christ is for us, and speaks as well of the features of this life (readiness to forgive enemies, a capacity for spiritual discernment, patience, kindness, humility,) he makes his point by telling us that we are to "put on" Christ with his gifts. "Put on" is a metaphor taken from the realm of clothing. We are to *clothe* ourselves in Christ and his gifts. Our clothing ourselves in this way tells everyone that we belong to him.

The man whose name had been "legion" is now clothed. He belongs to Jesus Christ; he belongs to Christ's people; he belongs to the wider community; he belongs to himself.

Right-minded. In Hebrew thought to be possessed of a right mind, a sound mind, is to be sane, to be sure, but also, even more profoundly, it's to have one's thinking formed and informed by the truth and reality of God.

Most people are sane now. Most people, however, aren't "right-minded" in that they don't think in conformity with the kingdom of God. If they are asked what is real, what is good, what they should trust, what they should pursue, what is central in life and what is peripheral; if they are asked these questions they can answer them all in only a few words: "Whatever promotes my plans for myself; whatever advances my self-interest; whatever makes my life easier and makes me self-satisfied."

Most people are sane; most people are not right-minded, not *righteous*-minded in terms of right relationship with Jesus Christ and right pursuit in conformity with this relationship. The thinking of most people isn't governed by any of this; it's governed by rationalization, rationalization that aids and abets their selfism.

The man whose name had been "legion" is restored both to sanity and to a manner of thinking that's now governed by one grand preoccupation: the reality of God, the truth of God, the kingdom of God; God's plan and purpose for him *here*; his pursuit of *this*. What governs his thinking now isn't thinly-disguised scheming connected with self-promotion; what governs his thinking now is a vision of the kingdom of God and a vocation to render this kingdom visible.

When our Lord says to any one of us today, "What's your name?", the answer he's looking for isn't "Bill" or "Beatrice." When he asks the question he already knows the answer, yet asks the question in any case in order to have *us* recognize and admit and own the truth about ourselves. He already knows that our name is, or has been, "legion", since there are so many of us. And of course he asks the question only in order that he might speak to us, touch us, and thereafter use us as citizens of his kingdom who are possessed of his truth and preoccupied with his purposes for us and others. In short, he asks us the question only because he ultimately wants to render us seated, clothed, and right-minded.

8

WHY WORRY?

"Look at the birds of the air: they neither sow nor reap nor gather into barns, and yet your heavenly Father feeds them. Are you not of more value than they? And which of you by being anxious can add one cubit to his span of life? And why are you anxious about clothing? Consider the lilies of the field, how they grow; they neither toil nor spin; yet I tell you, even Solomon in all his glory was not arrayed like one of these. But if God so clothes the grass of the field, which today is alive and tomorrow is thrown into the oven, will he not much more clothe you, O men of little faith? Therefore do not be anxious, saying, `What shall we eat?' or `What shall we drink?' or `What shall we wear?' For the Gentiles seek all these things; and your heavenly Father knows that you need them all. But seek first his kingdom and his righteousness, and all these things shall be yours as well. "Therefore do not be anxious about tomorrow, for tomorrow will be anxious for itself. Let the day's own trouble be sufficient for the day.

—Matthew 6:26-34

"Will worrying increase your life-expectancy?" asks Jesus. "Do you really think that worrying will let you live better or live longer? Then why are you anxious?" Upon hearing our Lord's question most of us find our anxiety—bad enough in itself—worsened now by guilt. After all, our Lord forbids us to worry and yet we continue to worry; in fact it seems we can't help worrying. Plainly we aren't measuring up to his word. We can only conclude that we're spiritually defective.

Then it's all the more important to understand from the outset that our Lord's word is meant to bring us relief and encouragement and hope. His word is never meant to bring us distress or despair. We should understand too that the anxiety of which he speaks in our scripture text isn't anxiety of every sort; specifically it's anxiety connected to acquisitiveness. *This* kind of anxiety is a spiritual problem. But not all anxiety is a spiritual problem. Some anxiety is a psychological problem.

Panic attacks, for instance, are a psychological afflicton. Panic attacks are a psychological disorder having nothing to do with one's spiritual condition. A panic attack is a sudden onset of overwhelming anxiety for no apparent reason. One minute someone feels fine; the next minute dread has iced her heart. Severe panic attacks are immobilizing—a clergyman standing in the pulpit on Sunday morning, suddenly unable to utter a word; a social worker looking into a department store window, suddenly unable to take a step; a man about to take his wife to a restaurant, suddenly unable to leave the house. As a pastor I have had all three cases brought to me. In all of these it must never be suggested that someone's faith is weak or that someone is a defective Christian.

If we wonder why some people are afflicted with panic attacks, we should also say, "Why do some people develop arthritis in their right knee? Why do some people develop astigmatism in their left eye? Why is it that when the Norwalk virus was going around two people out of ten came down with it, but only two?" Years ago I discovered, quite by accident, that I am slightly claustrophobic and somewhat colour blind. But none of this has anything to do with my spiritual condition.

We must never suggest that if only those who suffer from sudden onsets of panic had greater faith they would suffer no longer. We ought never to add guilt to their anxiety.

In the second place we should understand that another kind of anxiety is related to emotional injury. An able pastor whom I have known for years served in the Royal Navy during World War II. He was under fire dozens of times. Decades later he still wakes up in the night shouting, "My life jacket! Where's my life jacket? I can't find my life jacket!" His wife gets him up and they make tea. Then he goes to his study and commences work, since he knows he isn't going to sleep again that night.

There are civilian equivalents of this. People who have survived house fires, survived train wrecks, survived automobile manglings, survived childhood traumas of every sort (abuse included); these people are wounded emotionally. Anxiety surrounds their wound. This kind of anxiety isn't a sign of spiritual deficiency.

Moreover, the people who are afflicted with such anxiety display remarkable courage. It takes courage, immense courage, to keep stepping ahead in life when we know that the emotional landmine will blow up in our face from time to time. It takes courage to resist the temptation to self-pity. It takes courage to hobble or limp or stagger when everyone else seems to be galloping. It takes courage to keep moving ahead when virtually no one else understands us and our vulnerability to anxieties that appear to afflict few others. Such people can only be commended for their courage.

* * * *

If the kind of anxiety Jesus has in mind in our text isn't the kind we have mentioned so far, then what does Jesus mean when he says, "Don't be anxious; worrying won't help you live longer or live better"?

Our Lord has in mind the kind of anxiety we forge in ourselves when we persist in pursuing what isn't of God's kingdom. We persist in pursuing it and fear that we might not be able to get it, or fear that we might not be able to keep it, or fear that someone else might get the same thing thereby depriving us of our claim to distinction, even uniqueness, even superiority.

Jesus says, "Where your treasure is, there will your heart be also." In other words, what we really cherish (as opposed to what we say we cherish); this is that to which we are going to give ourselves; and this is that from which we are going to expect the greatest returns. Then what do we cherish?

The adolescent reads the bodybuilding advertisements. He starts "pumping iron," not because exercise is good and everyone should exercise to promote bodily (and mental) health; he "pumps iron" in that he thinks he's going to look like Arnold Schwarzenegger in six months. Once he's looking like "Hulk", all kinds of wonderful things are going to come his way. After six months he doesn't look much different. He thinks there's something wrong with him. He goes to his physician, who tells him there's nothing wrong with him, and tells him too that he's never going to look like a gorilla. The fellow disregards the advice and goes to a speciality store to buy pills and diet supplements guaranteed to maximize muscle.

Why does he want to look like "Mr. Big" in the first place? He wants to inasmuch as he has absorbed the cult of the physique from his society. Unhappy with his body image, he's determined to re-sculpt himself into an image that doesn't embarrass him. He's preoccupied with being pumped up just because the world at large is preoccupied with being puffed up. (Everything we've said about males and muscle we could say as readily about females and silicon and iron-pumping as well.)

Our concern with self-magnification and inflated ego fosters anxiety. Envy fosters anxiety. Lack of contentment fosters anxiety. Aware of the inverse relationship between contentment and anxiety, I'm always moved at the paintings of the Jewish artist, Hibel. Hibel paints the wisdom that has permeated the *shtetln* for centuries, the *shtetln* being the east European Jewish villages now consumed forever. My favourite painting is of a group of east European Jewish men in their fur-rimmed hats and long earlocks, together with wives in their kerchiefs, dancing and cavorting in irrepressible joy. Underneath are the words, "Who are rich? Those who rejoice in their portion."

Other matters breed in us the anxiety that's a sign of spiritual ill health. One such matter is a lack of singlemindedness concerning the kingdom of God or the truth of God or the righteousness of God. Any pastor regularly sees people whose anxiety has arisen over moral compromise. Now they are riding two horses at once. They could ride either one or the other, but to do this would mean giving up something. Then they might as well keep on riding both for a while—except that the two horses, the two paths, the two commitments are beginning to diverge and it appears that someone is going to be pulled apart. The apostle Paul reminds young Timothy, "No soldier on active service gets sidetracked in civilian pursuits." Exactly. Lack of singlemindedness concerning the kingdom of God, the truth of God, the righteousness of God; double-mindedness will always mire us in anxiety.

There's something else spiritually important that causes anxiety to surge over us and settle within us: our refusal to admit that life is fragile. Because we won't admit that life is fragile and therefore won't come to terms with its uncertainty, we preoccupy ourselves with rendering life 100% certain and secure, only to find that we can't; we can never domesticate life like this. The attempt at rendering life foolproof, accident-proof, disaster-proof, disease-proof, suffering-proof, surprise-proof; this attempt always fails in the end, but not before we have rendered ourselves anxious beyond telling and also warped ourselves profoundly. It's always better to admit that life is fragile; nothing is permanent; bodily security is impossible, and our true security, profound security, lies in God's care for us and our trust in his care. Many expressions in scripture point to life's fragility and impermanence: "All flesh is grass"; "The form of this world is passing away"; "We are dust"; "Our years are soon gone; they fly away." All these expressions mean the same: life is precarious. Yet the myth persists that life can be made perfectly secure. The preoccupation with making life secure merely makes us inwardly more insecure as anxiety multiplies.

* * * * *

The gospel insists, in the midst of our fragility and anxiety, that there *is* a security that can't be dislodged: "Seek first God's kingdom and God's righteousness," our Lord maintains. Whenever I lose sight of what I'm to be about first; whenever I lose sight of what *is* first, I'm corrected by "beaming up" one or two men with whom I appear to have little in common yet by whom I've been helped profoundly over and over: drug addicts or alcoholics who have been rendered contentedly sober by the grace of God. The AA man or woman who knows and cherishes contented sobriety knows, and knows from terrible experience, that the roof can be falling in anywhere or everywhere in life; still, no disruption can be allowed to threaten his sobriety. Yes, he may have lost his job; but the difficulties arising over losing his job won't be helped if he loses his job *and* his sanity. He may find the boss insufferable; but chemically induced oblivion won't rid the office of the boss. Of all the slogans that adorn the walls of the room where the AA meeting is held the three that speak so very tellingly to me are, "How important is it?" "First things first," and "It's not your drinking, it's your stinking thinking."

"How important is it?" However important "it" might be, it isn't so important as to be worth the surrender of one's sobriety and contentment.

"First things first." The man or woman's deliverance is plainly first and must be kept first just because it can't be relegated to second. The sober alcoholic knows that if his contented sobriety is ever moved down to second, it won't even be second for the simple reason that it won't exist at all.

"It's not your drinking; it's your stinking thinking." "Stinking thinking" is thinking that its perpetrator believes to be the soul of rationality and common sense, when any observer knows it to be self-serving rationalisation and lethal stupidity.

And therefore every day when concerns cascade upon me and threaten to multiply anxiety in me I have to recall the fact of God's kingdom and righteousness and my commitment to that kingdom and righteousness. And as often as I recall God's kingdom and righteousness, now threatened with being eclipsed by whatever has upset me, I have to say to myself as well, "How important is it? First things first. What you think to be pure rationality, Professor Shepherd, is the shabbiest rationalisation."

I have learned something more from my friends who have been substance abusers. They live for one thing: helping another suffering person to the same experience, the same truth. The AA member can be a farmer, a physician, a truck driver, a homemaker. At least this is how a livelihood is earned. Living, however, is something else. Living is now a matter of helping a suffering person with messed up head and heart towards a new day, a bright day; a day in whose light the old day, dark day, evil day is repudiated even as God is enjoyed and praised forever. In other words, my friends live to introduce someone else to that deliverance for which they are eternally grateful themselves.

I find myself challenged by all of this, and often rebuked by it. I'm impelled to ask myself again and again, "What *do* I live for? Do I live to help a fellow-sufferer and fellow-sinner with messed up head and heart towards a new day, a bright day in which God is known and God's reign becomes the atmosphere that sustains and satisfies even as God himself is praised forever? In other words, do *I* live to introduce someone else to that deliverance for which I am eternally grateful myself?

I can't avoid asking this question. After all, the fact that I'm called "reverend" doesn't mean I've entered that gate which Jesus pronounces narrow or embarked upon that way which Jesus calls rigorous. I have no doubt that the clergy's daily trafficking in religion can render any minister impervious to the gospel. And then perchance I meet the AA member whose eyes shine just because he's had, only yesterday, the opportunity of introducing someone to that blessing which only those who are acquainted with it can understand. I recall the word of our Lord: "Do you really want to be rid of your envious anxiety and your niggling moodiness and your childish resentment? Then seek *first* God's kingdom and God's righteousness. The other matters will soon sort themselves out."

A few verses before Jesus tells us to seek first God's kingdom and righteousness and therein shed our anxiety he says, "Don't lay up for yourselves treasure upon earth, where inflation erodes it and governments tax it. You lay up treasure in heaven, for where your treasure is, there will your heart be also." We've already seen what this means; namely, what we cherish is what we pursue. Immediately Jesus adds, "The eye is the lamp of the body; if your eye is sound, your whole body is full of light. But if your eye is unsound, your whole body is full of darkness."

The Greek word that our English Bible translates "sound" has two dictionary meanings: "single" and "generous." The Greek word that our English Bible translates "unsound" literally means "evil." "Evil eye" is a Hebrew expression that means grudging, miserly, stingy, ungenerous. According to Jesus to be miserly, stingy, ungenerous is to have our entire self darkened, while to be singleminded concerning God's kingdom and generous as well is to have our entire self full of light.

God has given himself to us without condition, without measure, without reservation. His "eye" has been sound in that he has been singleminded in his search for us and generous in lavishing himself upon us. His "eye" has never been an "evil eye"; that is, he has never been grudging, miserly, stingy. He calls us to be "sound-eyed" ourselves, giving ourselves to him and to those whom he brings before us. If our eye is sound, says Jesus, then we ourselves shall be full of light. If our eye is evil (i.e., if we are stingy and miserly) then we shall be dark ourselves and incapable of reflecting his light upon anyone else.

* * * * *

"Do you think that by worrying you can live ten minutes longer?" asks Jesus. "Then seek first God's kingdom and God's righteousness. Where your treasure is, your heart will be. If your eye is sound, your whole body will be full of light." This is our Lord's antidote to anxiety.

9

DO YOU ALSO WISH
TO GO AWAY?

So Jesus said to them, "Truly, truly, I say to you, unless you eat the flesh of the Son of man and drink his blood, you have no life in you; he who eats my flesh and drinks my blood has eternal life, and I will raise him up at the last day." . . . Many of his disciples, when they heard it, said, "This is a hard saying; who can listen to it?" But Jesus, knowing in himself that his disciples murmured at it, said to them, "Do you take offense at this? . . . After this many of his disciples drew back and no longer went about with him. Jesus said to the twelve, "Do you also wish to go away?" Simon Peter answered him, "Lord, to whom shall we go? You have the words of eternal life; and we have believed, and have come to know, that you are the Holy One of God."

—John 6:53-71

Crowds are fickle. Crowds are easily swayed. A rabble-rousing speech can turn a docile crowd into a dangerous mob in only minutes.

And even where a crowd isn't dangerous, a crowd can still be led to emote and act in a way that individuals in the crowd never would. Many of us need only recall the sober, sensible, middle-aged women who thronged Toronto's Nathan Phillips Square at the height of "Trudeau-mania." The prime minister (a man who drilled his children, "'Reason over emotion,' remember; 'reason over emotion'") turned these chaste matrons into a crowd of hero worshippers whose fantasy lives were never more heated.

At one point in my life I watched TV programs that aired debates. I noticed that the audience (a "crowd" of the sort we are discussing now) frequently reversed its opinion as it listened to a clever speaker overturn (as it were) what the audience had first upheld, only to reverse its opinion again as the second speaker, slightly more clever (but no more profound) overturned what had just been overturned. While I found such programs an amusing diversion, not to say a study in crowd psychology, at the same time I realized that democracy is exceedingly susceptible to demagoguery. In only a few minutes the clever wordsmith can have people doing publicly what they have vowed privately never to do.

Jesus attracted crowds, but he never trusted crowds. Crowds were numerous; followers remained few. Unlike demagogues or even wordsmiths, our Lord never manipulated people and therefore never "worked up" a crowd intentionally. On the other hand, even in his day a crowd was a crowd: however transparent and straightforward he might be, the crowd that was listening to him continued to behave like any other crowd. On one occasion a crowd found itself swept off its feet as he spoke; swept off its feet, that is, in that it was startled at him and impressed by him even as it misunderstood him. Its misunderstanding was glaring: it tried to make him king in conformity with its own distorted sense of ruler. The crowd wanted to make Jesus its revolutionary leader.

Jesus refused. He knew that while redressing social iniquities was important, the revolutionaries who clamour for justice today inasmuch as they are victims of injustice will visit injustice on others tomorrow as soon as they have access to the political power they've been denied. Jesus maintained that what matters above all is a new heart (the heart being, for Hebrew-schooled people, a person's "control centre" that integrates thinking, feeling, willing, and making judgements.) Jesus maintained too that the new heart entails as well a new road to be walked, new resources to be claimed, new confidence in God's future for his people.

Revolution is certainly understandable; revolution may sometimes be necessary (some people at least would say.) But while revolution changes the players in the game, making losers of winners and winners of losers, it never changes the game itself. It interchanges exploiter and exploited, victimizer and victim, prideful and resentful; it never transforms the human heart. Jesus knew that his purpose was to unloose the powers of the age to come, and this for the sake of having men and women "taste" the powers of the age to come, as Hebrews tells us graphically. Jesus refused to be heralded as the leader of the revolutionaries' revolution; he knew that at bottom the people's revolution is no more to be trusted than the tyrant's tyranny. Jesus never allowed himself to be sidetracked or co-opted.

Still, as long as he has a crowd in front of him he will address it. "Unless you eat my flesh and drink my blood, you have no life in you," he cries.

He seems not to be referring here primarily to Holy Communion. He's speaking, rather, of what Holy Communion points to and is a means to; namely, our most intimate union with him. "Unless you receive me, cherish me, abide in me as I abide in you, have me embedded in your bloodstream, you are spiritually inert, lifeless even."

Now the crowd's been roused; in fact it's livid. Who wants to be told she's as insensitive to God as a corpse? "This is a hard saying," the crowd gripes and grumbles; "Who can listen to it?" Actually, the apostle John doesn't say it's the crowd that gripes and grumbles, as the crowd would be expected to; it's "some of his disciples." In other words, even some of those people who have distinguished themselves from the crowd by being more than curiosity seekers, more than spectators; even some of those who have begun to follow Jesus resent what he's just said. These shallow followers who are little more than the crowd; they turn away from Jesus and melt back into that crowd which has already hardened its heart against him.

Crowds are fickle; if it likes what you say, you're a hero; if not, you're laughable. One minute the crowd hailed Jesus as the grand leader of the people's revolution; next minute the crowd, together with some of those who had emerged from the crowd and had begun to follow him, turned on him and turned away from him.

Jesus wasn't surprised. He looked at the twelve, those who knew him most intimately and insisted they had left everything to follow him; Jesus looked at them and said, "Do you want to leave too? Now's your chance." Speaking for the twelve Peter gasped, "Leave? Where could we go? To whom could we go? *You* have the words of eternal life."

* * * * *

The question Jesus put to the twelve he puts to us. "Do you wish to leave also?" As a matter of fact people *do* leave; they are leaving him all the time. Why?

95

Some people leave because they disagree vehemently with our Lord's assessment of humankind. They are irked, exasperated, finally angered when he persists in telling them, "Unless you eat my flesh and drink my blood; unless you receive me, the only saviour you can ever have, you have no life in you—none at all."

"But we are good people and we do good things. We've never been in jail; we pay income tax; we give $50 dollars per year to the United Way. We've never so much as harmed a gerbil." None of this is in doubt. Their moral rectitude is indisputable. And the tragedy is, their moral rectitude is the shield behind which they hide from God. Their virtue is the achievement they point to in order to "prove" that they don't need a saviour. Their goodness legitimates their flight from the God who wants to remedy the *sin* of the good and the bad alike.

They never see that their goodness, indisputably good, is still only a good veneer. In the wake of the Fall human goodness, virtue, rectitude; it's all no more than one millimetre thick. Civilization is one millimetre thick. Humanism is one millimetre thick. Once this epidermal layer is punctured, pus pours out: savagery, barbarism.

All of us have seen the pictures of the holocaust survivors at the end of World War II: emaciated, vacant, skeletal. We used to regard it as an aberration, a "one-off" event. Then in the '90s we saw the emaciated people in the Serbian prisoner of war camps; their ribs could be counted, their skulls so fleshless their eyeballs appeared on the point of falling out. A dear friend of mine, a Croatian Muslim woman ("Rosie") who owns and operates a coffee shop that I frequent, told me of her nieces and nephews in what used to be Yugoslavia. The children had been found with their throats cut.

And if perchance you see pictures from the earliest days of photography, pictures of Andersonville, Georgia, where Union prisoners of war were detained by Robert E. Lee's Confederate forces, you will notice that those men look exactly like the men and women from Auschwitz.

Elie Wiesel, himself a survivor of the holocaust (he was sent there when he was fifteen), appeared on TV in connection with the Yugoslavian atrocities. Sadly Wiesel commented, "In forty-five years humankind has learned nothing."

Of course it's learned nothing. Humankind learns nothing precisely because it disdains our Lord's "unless" and blithely continues to assume it needs to learn nothing.

We should notice that while the allies bombed everything connected with the German war effort that they could, they never bombed the railway tracks that conveyed doomed people to the death camps—even though the allies had known about these camps at least since 1943. Why not? Because we were glad enough to have someone else annihilate the people the world despises.

And while caucasian newcomers to North America indisputably harmed aboriginal peoples in many ways, caucasians didn't make aboriginals sinners. For thousands of years before one white person set foot in North America the aboriginals had refined torture not only as a means of extracting military information but also as a highly-desired form of entertainment.

"In forty-five years humankind has learned nothing" Wiesel ponders bewilderingly? He could have said, "For as long as human history lasts humankind won't learn anything."

Won't learn anything, that is, unless; "unless you eat my flesh and drink my blood...." To be sure, there's no lack of those itching to say that people who make a religious profession are no different. But Jesus doesn't urge us to parrot a religious profession. He urges us to come to him, live in him, absorb him with his truth and his life; and absorb his truth and his life for the sake of absorbing his way. And to do all of this not once but over and over as long as breath remains in us.

The bottom line in all this is whether or not we agree with our Lord's diagnosis of humankind. During the days of his earthly ministry some people found it too severe, a "hard saying, a difficult teaching." They left. Many people leave today for the same reason: they disagree with our Lord's assessment of the human heart.

Other people leave for a different reason. Adversity dashes cold water on their faith, and the flame of faith seems to flicker and go out. I should never make light of someone else's hardship, and never make light of what that hardship has done to her.

At the same time, I'm aware that some people appear to be struck by adversity every bit as heavy yet don't leave. I'm aware that moderate pain seems to induce some people to give up on our Lord while severe pain finds other people trusting him more than ever. I have no explanation here. I'm simply aware that some people feel that life's beatings have beaten out of them that faith which they once thought to possess them. The adversity that expels "faith", of course, need not be their own. It can be someone else's adversity that they have witnessed, or at least should be aware of. Let's not forget that one-quarter of all children under five throughout the world die from malnutrition or civil war.

There's a third reason why people leave: they are simply preoccupied. In his parable of the sower and the seed Jesus speaks of the seed of the Word of God that falls on thorny ground. "They do receive the Word," says Jesus, "but the cares of the world, the delight in riches and their craving for trinkets and toys choke the Word."

Most of us Canadians live in a sea of affluence. Ever since 1867, the year Canada became a nation-state, real wealth per capita has doubled every generation. My wife and I are twice as wealthy as our parents, four times as wealthy as our grandparents, and so on. In Canada real wealth per capita has doubled in every generation for 150 years.

Not only are we distracted by the trinkets and toys our wealth allows us to purchase; our wealth renders us superficial, satisfied and cocky. Superficiality and arrogant self-satisfaction will overtake any of us unless we understand the spiritual threat that surrounds us in our ever-growing affluence. In other words, while hardship induces some people to forsake Jesus Christ, "softship" induces others to leave. In North America we are far more likely to be seduced by "softship."

* * * * *

As the crowds and even some *followers* of Jesus desert him he turns to the twelve and asks, "Do you also wish to go away?" Peter's reply is swift and sure: "To whom shall we go? *You* have the words of eternal life." Immediately Peter adds, "We have believed, and have come to *know*, that you are the holy one of God." The Greek verb tenses have to be read carefully here. Peter's reply has this force: "We have come to believe, *and now stand firm*; we have come to know, *and our conviction is unshakeable*, that you are the holy one of God, you have the words of eternal life, and it would be the height of folly for us to look anywhere else."

Many of us are so very turned off by the religious know-it-all that we assume unthinkingly it's better to be a know-nothing-at-all. But it isn't better. While the know-it-all is certainly obnoxious, the know-nothing-at-all is simply unhelpful. Peter and the others weren't parading themselves as know-it-alls when he spoke for them; yet they were just as far from being know-nothing-at-alls. "We know, our conviction is unshakeable, that *you* are the one our hearts fit and our heads meet and our hands must ever hold."

It's our experience of our Lord, tested in so many fires and shining ever more brightly, that gives us something to say and do and be. Without such experience of Jesus Christ all we can do is listen to other people's fear and superficiality and hopelessness and then reflect it all back to them. If we are going to be that light "which gives light to all in the house", according to Jesus, then we must enlighten; and this we can do only as we are first constrained to say with Peter, "We have come to believe, and we *know*...."

In the last several years I've noticed that the older I become the more sense the gospel makes. When I was younger I seemed to find problems, many problems, different kinds of problems, surrounding the gospel. Now the gospel strikes me as transparently sensible. Yet I have to admit that my experience here is precisely the opposite of our society's. Secularism means that the gospel makes less and less sense to neighbours near and far, less and less sense to our society as a whole. Still, while the church is proportionately smaller in our society than heretofore, the church can nonetheless have an effective place. Despite its smaller size the church will have an effective place in our society, however, only as the gospel first makes more and more sense to the *church*, only if we who endorse the gospel find ourselves constrained to say with Peter, "We have come to know, with unshakeable conviction, that *you* are God's presence and power, *you* have the words of eternal life. We have validated this in our own experience time without end, and we wouldn't think of looking anywhere else."

* * * * *

Let's return for a minute to the three kinds of people who leave off following our Lord.

First are those who are irked by his diagnosis concerning the savagery of the sinful human heart. Here we can only wait for the day when life leads them to see that his diagnosis happens to be correct. And because correct, it isn't oppressively negative but is wonderfully positive since it's the first step in their recovery.

Third are those whom "softship" has preoccupied. We can only wait until a shaft of light and truth shines so brightly that it pierces the fluffy insulation of their "softship" and strikes home.

Second are those whom adversity has trampled. Here there's much we can do. Gentleness and sensitivity are needed at all times. Concrete help may be in order much of the time. In it all they will know that we haven't abandoned them. Our not leaving them in their adversity will be a sign, *the* sign, that Jesus Christ hasn't abandoned them either. Knowing this, they will leave off leaving off, and will follow him, along with us.

For when our Lord turns to us and asks, "Do you also wish to go away?" We already know the answer we are going to give. "Why would we look anywhere else? We *know* that you are truth, way, and life."

10

...WOULD YOU BETRAY THE SON OF MAN WITH A KISS?

While he was still speaking, there came a crowd, and the man called Judas, one of the twelve, was leading them. He drew near to Jesus to kiss him; but Jesus said to him, "Judas, would you betray the Son of man with a kiss?" And when those who were about him saw what would follow, they said, "Lord, shall we strike with the sword?" And one of them struck the slave of the high priest and cut off his right ear. But Jesus said, "No more of this!" And he touched his ear and healed him. Then Jesus said to the chief priests and officers of the temple and elders, who had come out against him, "Have you come out as against a robber, with swords and clubs? When I was with you day after day in the temple, you did not lay hands on me. But this is your hour, and the power of darkness."

—Luke 22:47-53

"O that you would kiss me with the kisses of your mouth, for your love is better than wine." "Your kisses [are] like the best wine that goes down smoothly, gliding over lips and teeth." (Song of Solomon 1:2; 7:9). The Bible is always earthy in its discussion of sex. The world, on the other hand, tends to be vulgar, and ever more vulgar, in its discussion. Rightly offended at the world's vulgarity, the church reacts but too often reacts unhelpfully: offended because the world renders sex vulgar, the church then renders it ethereal, abstract, unearthly and unearthy.

Let's approach the matter from a different angle. We'll be helped as we ponder the difference between the erotic and the pornographic. The world often wallows in the pornographic, depicting sex as passion *only* without reference to persons. The church, on the other hand, often flees into a false spirituality by speaking of sex as a spiritual event without reference to passion.

The Hebrew mind is wiser than all of this. The Hebrew mind (and heart) knows that while the pornographic is humanly debasing, the erotic is humanly fulfilling. While the pornographic is perverse, the erotic is God-given. While the pornographic exploits, the erotic enhances. The Hebrew mind always remembers that it is *God* who has made us sexually differentiated. Therefore to denounce the erotic is to disdain the wisdom and goodness of God; it's to call "bad" what he has called "blessing." This, of course, is sin. The writer of the book of Proverbs was acquainted with the mind and will and purpose of God when he wrote that "the way of a man with a maid" is so marvellous as to transcend human comprehension. To be sure, he knew that the pornographic is eroticism debased, eroticism perverted, eroticism exploited, something good bent to an evil purpose, a blessing rendered a curse. Still, the fact of distortion and perversion never obliterates the goodness of God's intention and purpose. Where sexual matters are concerned, the Hebrew outlook is neither vulgar nor ethereal but instead earthy, God-glorifyingly earthy. "Your kisses are like the best wine that goes down smoothly, gliding over lips and teeth."

At the same time, because of its honesty and transparency scripture admits that *this* kiss can be perverted. The kiss of the seductress in Proverbs 7:13 is such a perversion. This woman, "dressed as a harlot, wily of heart" (7:10) kisses a fellow saying, "Let us take our fill of love till morning; let us delight ourselves with love. For my husband is not at home; he has gone on a long journey" (7:18-19). At the end of the day, however, the *distortion* of what is good cannot *deny* what is good. "O that you would kiss me with the kisses of your mouth."

Another feature of the Hebrew mind: it never pretends that the romantic kiss, the erotic kiss, is the only kind of kiss, or even the most important kind of kiss. Far more frequently scripture speaks of the kiss of parent and child, brother and sister, mother-in-law and daughter-in-law, even friend and friend.

Then we must examine other kisses, even hanker after other kinds of kisses, like the kiss with which Esau forgave his brother Jacob. Jacob was a scoundrel. His name, in Hebrew, means "deceiver", and he was as bad as his name. He deceived his father Isaac and defrauded his brother Esau. Jacob didn't pilfer nickels and dimes from Esau; Jacob plundered him. Jacob stole everything from Esau that there was to steal.

Jacob and Esau went their separate ways only to meet up years later. When Jacob was about to meet his brother he gathered up gifts without number hoping thereby to placate Esau and defuse Esau's retaliation. In other words, having displayed the cruellest cunning Jacob now displayed the crassest manipulation. At the moment of their meeting, however, Esau *didn't* slay Jacob. Esau didn't even demand compensation from Jacob. Instead, we are told, "Esau *ran* to meet Jacob, and embraced him, and fell on his neck, and kissed him, and they wept." Jacob, overwhelmed at Esau's forgiveness, cried, "Truly, to see your face is like seeing the face of God, with such favour have you received me" (Genesis 33:10).

Esau kisses Jacob in forgiveness; Jacob's heart melts at the unexpected magnanimity; he cries, "To see your face *is like seeing the face of God*, with such favour have you received me."

The Bible as a whole insists that no one can see the face of God and survive. Moses is permitted to look upon God's "backside", as it were, but not even Moses can see God's face—if he wants to survive. The closest any of us can come to seeing God's face is to see what is *like* God's face. And what is *like* God's face, the old story tells us, is the face of Esau as he pardons his brother, and more than merely pardons him; as he pours out such affection on Jacob as Jacob has never known, as he's so glad to see his brother that he's not even thinking of all he's lost, as he's so thrilled with the reconciliation—never mind who did what to whom—that he's oblivious to everything except the grand fact of having his brother back. Heedless of everything except his brother, Esau kisses Jacob—with the result that while Jacob, of course, has never seen the face of God, seeing Esau is *like* seeing the face of God.

Esau's kind of kissing is a most important kind. It's a kind of kissing we should come to be good at ourselves. After all, the people whom we meet in the spirit of Esau—the spirit of forgiveness—are people who will find that seeing our face is like seeing the face of God.

* * * * *

While we are talking about the kissing we must do we should also talk about the kissing we *mustn't* do. Judas betrayed his Lord with a kiss. (Mark 14:43-45) This is treachery. For years I thought there could be nothing worse than abandonment. Everyone is aware of the damage (frequently irreparable damage) visited upon children whose parents abandon them. Everyone has seen people abandoned by friends (or by those thought to be friends.) Everyone has seen someone courageously take a stand only to have that person's colleagues, having promised support, slink away in self-interest. For years, therefore, I thought there could be nothing worse than abandonment. I was wrong. There *is* something worse than abandonment: betrayal. What could be worse than treachery at the hands of those we have trusted?

Judas wasn't the first person in Israel's history to betray someone with a kiss. Towards the end of David's life David himself was in a sorry state; so were the people; so was the army. Amasa was the army's leader. Joab wanted the position. Upon meeting Amasa, one day, Joab grasped Amasa's beard and drew Amasa to himself so as to kiss him. Amasa never saw the knife in Joab's other hand. At the moment that Joab kissed Amasa, he disembowelled him. (2 Samuel 20:9) Judas kissed Jesus and thereby identified him for our Lord's killers. Like Joab, like Judas.

Like Joab, like John Smith. Like Joab, like Jane Doe. Treachery happens all the time. As terrible as abandonment is, there's something worse: betrayal.

There's a kiss we must ever abhor: the phoney kiss, the hollow kiss, the hypocritical kiss, the kiss of betrayal. How terrible is this kiss? Jesus said of Judas, "It would have been better for that man if he had never been born."

And then there's the kiss that moves me as often as I read of it. There was once a woman who learned that Jesus was lunching in the neighbourhood (Luke 7:36-52). She hadn't been invited to lunch. The host giving the lunch was Simon the Pharisee, and Pharisees didn't customarily invite to lunch those whose reputation was as discoloured as this woman's. Besides, Jesus and Simon were both men, and in first century Palestine men didn't talk to women in public.

Plainly the woman was overwhelmed with gratitude to Jesus and love for him as well. Initially it was gratitude: he had done for her what no one else had or could. Then it was love born of gratitude, even as the gratitude remained. Now love, gratitude, affection—all of it hugely magnified—together coursed through her as she forgot herself before the master.

Forgot herself? She never forgot herself. She knew exactly what she was doing at every minute. She wasn't invited to lunch but intruded herself anyway. She knew that men didn't talk to unknown women but threw herself upon Jesus in any case. She knew that letting down her hair in public was a disgrace for a woman (akin to denuding herself in public), but she didn't know what else to do to tell him she now had nothing to hide from him. Then she kissed his feet.

What a glorious reversal this was of the foot-kissing that had always been the oriental equivalent of bootlicking. In the eastern world of old, conquered kings, representing their conquered peoples, had to kiss the feet of their conqueror. It was an enforced public humiliation; it announced abject submission to that conqueror whom you hated but before whom you now had to grovel. To be defeated was bad enough; to have to acknowledge it publicly, worse; to have to acknowledge it by grovelling—bootlicking, foot-kissing—worst of all. (Isaiah 49:23)

How different it was with the woman who stole into the house of Simon the Pharisee. *She* wasn't defeated; she was freed. *She* wasn't forced into public humiliation; she was grateful. *She* wasn't grovelling before someone she loathed; she was rendering a service to someone she loved.

The woman kissed our Lord's feet. Plainly his feet didn't repel her. Plainly she thought his feet beautiful. "How beautiful are the feet" (we're quoting now from Isaiah 52); "how beautiful upon the mountains are the feet of him who brings good tidings, who publishes peace (*shalom*, salvation), who says to Zion, 'Your God reigns.'"

"How beautiful are the feet of him who brings good tidings." The prophet who penned these words had in mind Israel's tortuous exile, Israel suffering miserably at the hands of the Babylonians. Thanks to the Word of the Lord vouchsafed to him the prophet announced unequivocally that Israel's exile was ending: "We're going home!" And the people had exulted with one voice, "We're going home!"

When the woman kissed the beautiful feet of Jesus she had already come to know that he was more than the messenger of God; he was the message incarnate. She had already come to know that he wasn't telling her she was going home or even how to get home; in his company she *was* at home, and *knew* it.

One day when I was visiting a friend I asked her, just before the church-service began, what her favourite hymn was. Now my friend's upbringing had included an indifferent attitude toward the church. Upon marrying she had become a zealous believer and worked tirelessly in her congregation. Because her church background was as indifferent as mine was intense, I expected her to tell me that her favourite hymn was "Onward, Christian Soldiers" or some such "golden oldie" that any middle-aged Canadian would know of. In the course of replying to my question my friend stared ahead of her for the longest time and then said ever so softly, "My favourite hymn is 'Jesus see me at thy *feet*; nothing but thy blood can save me.'" Plainly she understands the woman who unpinned her hair and kissed the feet of Jesus.

* * * * *

When Simon the Pharisee objected strenuously to the poor taste of this uninvited woman Jesus said, "Simon, you never kissed me; it's plain you don't love much."

And then of course there's the "holy kiss" or the "kiss of love" (both expressions are used: Romans 16:16; 1 Peter 5:14) with which Christians are to greet each other. Over and over the epistles of the newer testament conclude with the reminder that Christians are to greet each other with a holy kiss or a kiss of love. We need not press it literally, any more than we are going to say that everyone should literally kiss the feet of Jesus. Still, the kiss with which Christians greet each other is important. In Israel friends kissed friends (David and Jonathan) as a sign of solidarity and affection, usually kissing each other on the forehead or the cheek or the shoulder. Today we shake hands or embrace.

In the Middle Ages men carried their weapon in their right hand. To shake hands with your right hand meant that you hadn't concealed even the smallest weapon and therefore weren't about to stab the person before you. In the ancient world, prior to the Middle Ages, soldiers carried their shield in their left hand. To shake hands with your left hand (like a Boy Scout) meant that you had discarded your shield and therefore weren't preoccupied with defending yourself.

What about shaking hands with both hands? Do we ever do it? Surely when we embrace we are shaking hands with both hands. Then to embrace means both hands are empty. We aren't concerned to attack or defend; we are simply going to *be*.

In the early church the holy kiss was exchanged immediately before Holy Communion. The Lord's Supper is an anticipation of the messianic banquet where savagery and treachery and betrayal, retaliation and vindictiveness and every kind of lethal one-upmanship will have no place and won't be found. Then they have no place in congregational life, and shouldn't be found there.

We needn't care whether someone kisses us, hugs us, shakes our hand, winks at us, or punches us on the shoulder— as long as we know that it's a holy punch or a holy wink and therefore we need neither attack nor defend; we need only *be*.

Lastly, all of us not only long to kiss; we also long to be kissed. Consider what it is to be kissed by God. The rabbis who came to the fore at the close of the Hebrew Bible used to say there are 103 ways of dying. Some deaths are relatively easy: we slip away peacefully in our sleep. Other deaths are more difficult. Some deaths are distressing. And some deaths, as every pastor and physician knows, are simply hideous. The easiest kind of death, slipping away in one's sleep, the rabbis spoke of as being "kissed by God."

The book of Hebrews maintains that Jesus Christ has "tasted" death for us. He has drunk death down, all of it, even at its most hideous; he has drunk it down so thoroughly as to drink it all up. Most profoundly, he has drunk up all the dregs of death so as to leave nothing in the cup for us to drink. Therefore the only death that remains for Christ's people is that death which in fact is to be kissed by God, *regardless of the circumstances of our dying.* To be sure, from a physical or psychological standpoint some deaths are easier than others. From a spiritual standpoint, however, all of Christ's people have been appointed to a death that is simply to be kissed by God.

* * * *

In view of the distressing deaths to which many martyrs have had to submit, can it be said of them that they were God-kissed? In light of all that we've noted about kissing and the different kinds of kissing, we should ask about Valentine, a martyr in the early church. We don't know exactly when he was born or when he died. We do know, however, that by the year 350 a church had been named after him in Rome. We know too that ever since the Middle Ages February 14 has been Valentine's feast day.

Since Valentine died the death of a martyr his death couldn't have been easy. In another respect, however, since he was one of Christ's own, he too died with the kiss of God upon him.

The rabbis of old maintained that Moses was the first to die by means of God's kiss. Moses may have been the first, but he certainly wasn't the last, for all Christ's people have been appointed to such a transition.

"Would you betray me with a kiss?" our Lord asks. So far from betraying him, we want only to be found in the company of the woman who knew she owed him everything and consequently fell at his feet, pouring out everything.

"Jesus, see me at thy feet; nothing but thy blood *has* saved me."

11

WHAT DID YOU EXPECT TO FIND?

Jesus began to speak to the crowds concerning John: "What did you go out into the wilderness to behold? A reed shaken by the wind? Why then did you go out? To see a man clothed in soft raiment? Behold, those who wear soft raiment are in kings' houses. Why then did you go out? To see a prophet? Yes, I tell you, and more than a prophet. This is he of whom it is written, 'Behold, I send my messenger before thy face, who shall prepare thy way before thee.' Truly, I say to you, among those born of women there has risen no one greater than John the Baptist; yet he who is least in the kingdom of heaven is greater than he. From the days of John the Baptist until now the kingdom of heaven has suffered violence, and men of violence take it by force. For all the prophets and the law prophesied until John; and if you are willing to accept it, he is Elijah who is to come. He who has ears to hear, let him hear."

—Matthew 11:7-15

We expect to find a family resemblance among relatives. John and Jesus were cousins. Not surprisingly, then, they were "look-alikes" in many respects.

Both were at home in the wilderness, the venue of extraordinary temptation and trial and testing, but also the venue of extraordinary intimacy with the Father.

Both preached out-of doors when they began their public ministry.

Both gave their disciples a characteristic prayer. John gave his followers a prayer that outwardly identified them as his disciples and inwardly welded them to each other. In no time the disciples of Jesus asked him for the same kind of characteristic prayer, with the result that we shall never be without the "Lord's Prayer."

Both John and Jesus lashed hearers whenever they spoke of God's severity and the inescapability of God's judgement.

Both summoned people to repent.

Both discounted the popular notion that God favoured Israel with political or national pre-eminence.

Both were born through an uncommon act of God.

And both died through having provoked uncommon rage among men and women.

John insisted that the sole purpose of his mission was to point away from himself to his younger cousin, Jesus. Jesus, for his part, never uttered one negative word about John. Jesus even endorsed John's ministry by submitting to baptism at John's hand. Indeed Jesus said, "Among those born of women (that is, of all the people in the world), there is none greater than John."

* * * * *

Elizabeth and Zechariah named their long-awaited son "Yochan." "Yochan" means "gift of God." This gift, however, didn't come with the pretty ribbons and bows and curlicues of fancy gift-wrapping. This gift came in a plain brown wrapper.

Think of John's appearance. He wore a camel-hide wrap-around, and it stank as only camels can stink. (Jesus, by contrast, wore a robe fine enough that soldiers gambled for it.)

Then there was John's diet: wild honey. How many bee stings did he have to endure to procure the honey? No doubt he had been stung so many times he was impervious, bees being now no more bothersome to him than fruit flies. And the locusts? There's lots of protein in grasshoppers, since small creatures like grasshoppers are the most efficient in converting grain protein into animal protein. Grasshoppers are good to eat, as long as you don't mind crunching their long legs and occasionally getting them stuck in your teeth. John was anything but effete, anything but dainty, anything but a reed shaken by the wind.

John's habitat was noteworthy. The wilderness, everywhere in Scripture, is the symbol for a radical break with the posturing and the pretence, the falsehoods and phoniness of the big city and its inherent corruption. Jerusalem, *hier shalem*, describes itself as the city of salvation. But is it? Jerusalem kills the prophets and crucifies the Messiah. By living in the wilderness John contradicted everything the city represented.

And of course there was John's manner. He had relatively few tools in his toolbox. When he saw that the truth of God had to be upheld and the sin of the powerful rebuked, he reached into his toolbox and came up with its one and only tool: confrontation. It wasn't long before he con-

WHAT DID YOU EXPECT TO FIND?

fronted Herodias, wife of Herod the ruler. John looked her in the eye and said, "First you married Phillip, your *uncle* Phillip, no less. Then you 'fooled around' with the man who is currently your husband. Then you allowed your daughter, Salome, to dance like a stripper in order to inflame a crowd of half-drunk military officers. You, Mrs. Herod, are incestuous, adulterous, and a pimp all at once. It's an abomination to God; you yourself are a disgrace; and the stench of it all looms larger than a mushroom cloud." Whereupon Mrs. Herod had said, "I'll have your head for that. Watch me."

We mustn't forget John's singlemindedness. Because his camel-hide loincloth lacked pockets, John kept his one-and-only sermon in his head and his heart. It was a simple sermon. The judgement of God is so close at hand that even now you can feel God's fiery breath scorching you and withering everything about you that can't stand the conflagration. And in the face of this judgement, thundered John, there are three things that cosy, comfortable people think they can take refuge in when there is no refuge; namely, parentage, piety and prestige.

Parentage. "Abraham is our parent. We are safe because we are descendants from the grand progenitor of our people, Abraham our father." We are Abraham's son or daughter only if we have Abraham's faith, John knew. In light of the crisis that God's judgement brings on everyone, we're silly for putting stock in the fact that our grandmother was once a missionary in China and our father once shook hands with Billy Graham.

Piety. "We are Israelites. Only last week we had our son circumcised." "We've been members of St.Matthew's-by-the-Gas Station for forty years. We had all our children 'done' there; we also contributed to the repairs to the steeple." Piety, said John, is a religious inoculation. Like any inoculation it keeps people from getting the real thing. For this reason piety is worse than useless: it guarantees that what *can* save us we shall never want.

Prestige. "We are the Jerusalem aristocrats." In 18th Century England an aristocrat was asked what she thought of John Wesley's movement. "A perfectly horrid thing," the Duchess of Buckingham had replied, turning up her nose as if someone had just taken the lid off an 18th Century chamber pot; "Imagine being told you are as vile as the wretches that crawl about on the earth."

It was little wonder that those who found John too much to take eased their discomfort by ridiculing him. *Baptizein* is the everyday Greek verb meaning to dip or to dunk—"John the dipper. "Well, Yochan, what'll it be today? Dunk your doughnuts or dip your paintbrush? Here comes the dippy dunker."

Might John have been deranged? His enemies said he was crazy. But the same people who said John was crazy said Jesus was an alcoholic. Certainly John was crude. Jesus admitted as much when he told those whom John had shocked, "What did you expect to see? A reed shaken by the wind? A feeble fellow smelling of perfume?" John lacked the polish of the cocktail crowd. But he was sane.

* * * * *

Regardless of the family resemblance between John and Jesus they're not identical.

John came to bear witness to the light. Jesus *was* (and is) that light.

John pointed to Jesus as the coming one. Jesus pointed to *himself* as the Incarnate one.

John reminded the people of God's centuries-old promises. Jesus was, and is, the *fulfilment* of all God's promises.

John administered a baptism of water as an outward sign of repentance. Jesus administered a baptism of fire as the Spirit inwardly torched his people.

The lattermost point highlights the crucial difference between John and Jesus. John could only *point* to the kingdom of God, the all-determining reality that was to heal a creation disfigured by the Fall. Jesus, on the other hand, didn't point to it: he *brought* it inasmuch as he *was* the new creation, fraught with cosmic significance, the one in whom all things are restored. John's ministry prepared people for a coming kingdom that the king would bring with him. Jesus' ministry gathered people into that kingdom which was operative wherever the king himself presided—which is to say, everywhere.

It's not that Jesus contradicted John. Rather, Jesus effected within people what John could only hold out for them. Because the ministry of Jesus gathered up the ministry of John, nothing about John was lost. At the same time, the ministry of Jesus contained so much more than John's—as John himself gladly admitted. In other words, the ministry of Jesus was the ministry of John *plus* all that was unique to our Lord.

Ponder, for instance, the note of repentance sounded by both men. John thundered. He threatened. There was a bad time coming, and John, entirely appropriately, had his hearers scared. Jesus agreed. There *is* a bad time coming. Throughout the written gospels we find on the lips of Jesus pronouncements every bit as severe as anything John said. Nonetheless, Jesus promised a good time coming too. To be sure, Jesus could flay the hide off phoneys as surely as John, yet flaying didn't *characterize* him; mercy did. While Jesus could speak, like John, of a coming judgement that couldn't be avoided, Jesus also spoke of an amnesty, a provision, a refuge that reflected the heart of his Father. Everything John said, the whole world needs to hear. Yet we need to hear even more urgently what Jesus alone said: "There's a party underway, and at this party all who are weary and worn down, frenzied and fed up, overwhelmed and overrun—at this party all such people are going to find rest and restoration, help, healing and hope."

Jesus, like John, spoke to the defiant self-righteous who not only disdained entering the kingdom themselves but also, whether deliberately or left-handedly, impeded others from entering it; Jesus, too, spoke to these people in a vocabulary that would take the varnish off a door. Jesus, however, also had his heart broken over people who were like sheep without a shepherd, about to follow cluelessly the next religious hireling—the religious "huckster" of any era who exploits the most needy and the most defenceless.

Because John's message was the penultimate word of judgement, the mood surrounding John was as stark, spare, ascetic as John's word: he drank no wine and he ate survival rations. Because Jesus' message was the ultimate word of the kingdom, the mood surrounding Jesus was the mood of a celebration, a party. He turned 150 gallons of water into wine—a huge amount for a huge party. He is the wine of life; he profoundly gladdens the hearts of men and women.

With his laser vision Jesus stared into the hearts of those who faulted him and said, "You spoil-sports with shrivelled hearts and acidulated tongues; you wouldn't heed John because his asceticism left you thinking he wasn't sane. Now you won't heed me because my partying leaves you thinking I'm not moral. Still, those people you've despised and duped and defrauded: your victims are victors now; they're going to be vindicated. And their exuberance in the celebrations they have with me not even your sullenness can diminish." Whereupon our Lord turned from the scornful snobs that religion forever breeds and welcomed yet another wounded, worn-down person who wouldn't know a hymnbook from a homily yet knew as much as she needed to know: life in the company of Jesus is indescribably better than life in the company of his detractors.

I'm always moved at our Lord's simple assertion, "I am the good shepherd." What did he mean by "good"? Merely that he is a competent shepherd, as any competent shepherd can protect the flock against marauders, thieves and disease? There are two Greek words for "good": *agathos* and *kalos*. *Agathos* means "good" in the sense of upright, proper, correct. *Kalos*, on the other hand (the word Jesus used of himself), includes everything that *agathos* connotes plus "winsome, attractive, endearing, appealing, compelling, comely, inviting." *I am the fine shepherd.*

Malcolm Muggeridge accompanied a film crew to India in order to narrate a documentary on the late Mother Teresa. He already knew she was a good woman or he wouldn't have bothered going. When he met her, however, he found a good woman who was also so very compelling, wooing, endearing that he titled his documentary, *Something Beautiful for God.*

John was good, *agathos*. Many people feared him and many admired him. Jesus was good, *kalos*. Many people feared him, many admired him, and *many loved him*. Paul speaks in Ephesians 6:24 of those who "love our Lord with love undying." Did anyone *love* John with love undying? If we've grasped the difference between *agathos* and *kalos*, between what is good, correct, upright and what is so very inviting and attractive as to be beautiful, then we've grasped the relation of John to Jesus.

There's another dimension to Jesus that carries him beyond John. It's reflected in the word he used uniquely at prayer, *abba*, "Father." Now the Newer Testament is written in Greek, even though Jesus customarily spoke Aramaic. In other words what our Lord said day-by-day has been translated into another language. Then why wasn't the Aramaic word, *abba*, translated into Greek? The word was left untranslated in that Jesus had first used it in a special way, and to translate it would seem to sully its distinctiveness.

Abba was the word used by a Palestinian youth to speak of his or her father respectfully, obediently, confidently, securely, and of course intimately. It wasn't so "palsy walsy" as to be disrespectful. Neither was it so gushing as to be sentimental. It was intimate without being impertinent, confident without being smug. *Abba* was trusting one's father without trading on the father's trustworthiness, familiar without being forward, secure without being saccharine.

We must be sure to understand that when early-day Christians came to use the word *abba* in their prayers they weren't repeating the word just because they knew Jesus had used it and they thought it cute to imitate him. Neither were they mumbling it mindlessly like a mantra thinking that if they kept on saying it, mantra-like, whatever it was within him that had given rise to it would eventually appear within them. On the contrary, they were impelled to use the word for one reason: as companions of Jesus they had been admitted to such an intimacy with the Father that the word Jesus had used uniquely of his Father they were now constrained to use too, so closely did their intimacy resemble his. When Paul writes in Romans 8:15 that Christians can't help uttering the cry, "*Abba*, Father", any more than a person in pain can help groaning or a person bereaved can help weeping or a person tickled by a good joke can help laughing; when Paul reminds the

Christians in Rome that this is normal Christian experience, "normal" means being introduced by the Son to the Father in such a way and at such a depth that the Son's intimacy with the Father induces the believer's intimacy. *Abba.*

We should note that the written gospels show us that Jesus used this word in Gethsemane; Gethsemane, of all places, when he was utterly alone at the most tormented hour of his life. I understand this. William Stringfellow, Harvard-taught lawyer and self-taught theologian who went to Harlem in a store-front law practice on behalf of the impoverished people he loved; Stringfellow, ridiculed by his denomination, suspected by the Kennedys and arrested finally by the FBI for harbouring Daniel Berrigan (a Jesuit anti-Viet Nam War protester); Stringfellow wrote in a little confirmation class book he prepared for teenagers, "Prayer is being so alone that God is the only witness to your existence."

The day comes for all of us when we are so thoroughly alone we couldn't be more alone. And in the isolation and torment of such a day we are going to find that God *is* the only witness to our existence. But he will be witness enough. And because it's the *Father* who is the only witness to our existence, we shall find ourself crying spontaneously, *"Abba."* Surely Jesus had this in mind when he said, "There has never appeared anyone greater than John the Baptist. Yet the least in the kingdom is greater than John."

We all need to be shaken up by the wild man from the wilderness, the grasshopper-eating, hide-wearing prophet whom no one should have mistaken for a reed shaken by the wind. Yet as often as we need to look at John, we find fearsome John pointing away from himself to Jesus, the Word Incarnate, the Lamb of God and the Saviour of the world; someone no less rigorous than John to be sure, but also so much more than John— someone so very winsome, compelling, inviting as to be *beautiful.*

HOW CAN YOU BELIEVE?

"Truly, truly, I say to you, unless one is born anew, he cannot see the kingdom of God." Nicodemus said to him, "How can a man be born when he is old? Can he enter a second time into his mother's womb and be born?" Jesus answered, "Truly, truly, I say to you, unless one is born of water and the Spirit, he cannot enter the kingdom of God. That which is born of the flesh is flesh, and that which is born of the Spirit is spirit. Do not marvel that I said to you, 'You must be born anew.' The wind blows where it wills, and you hear the sound of it, but you do not know whence it comes or whither it goes; so it is with every one who is born of the Spirit." Nicodemus said to him, "How can this be?" Jesus answered him, "Are you a teacher of Israel, and yet you do not understand this? Truly, truly, I say to you, we speak of what we know, and bear witness to what we have seen; but you do not receive our testimony. If I have told you earthly things and you do not believe, how can you believe if I tell you heavenly things?"

—John 3:1-12

"Earthly things" are everyday matters that can be seen as creaturely only, or can also be seen as analogous to matters of the Spirit. Physical birth is one such "earthly thing." It can be taken as no more than a fact of nature, or understood to be a symbol of another, different sort of, begetting. "Heavenly things" are matters that may unfold in the context of everyday creatureliness but in truth are rooted in the salvific action of God. If Nicodemus can't apprehend the former, how much less likely is he to grasp the latter. It's no surprise, then, that when Jesus had spoken of being "born again" Nicodemus had remained uncomprehending.

Without doubt "born again" (or "born anew") are fighting words. As soon as these words are sounded today people choose sides; people are polarized, and from their position (which position they will defend ardently) they contend vehemently.

In one corner are those for whom the words "born again" are a badge of identification to be worn unashamedly. If others don't use the expression, or don't use it as frequently as they salt and pepper their food; if others are thereby thought not to support instantaneous conversion arising from a crisis, then they are deemed not to be Christians at all.

In the other corner are those who minimize the element of crisis while maximizing the need for nurture. They insist that people become Christians through a steady process of nurture. Often they maintain that their approach is the only sensible one. If others disagree, they smile condescendingly and suggest that all who disagree lack social sophistication and intellectual profundity.

One group suggests that if we don't use the words "born again" we lack spiritual authenticity. The other group suggests that if we do use the words we lack intellectual substance.

When the fighting words "born again" bring out religious nastiness (as they often do, regrettably), the "nurturists" point to a few "born againers" who are manifestly emotionally unstable. The truth is, all of us are acquainted with someone who wields the expression "born again" like a hammer even as his psychological balance is precarious. On the other hand the "born againers" remind the nurturists that what often passes for Christian nurture is so very dilute that it wouldn't nurture a chickadee. And besides, they add, what can nurture do for stillbirths?

These latter people have a point. On my first pastoral charge the Sunday School lacked teachers. But this was thought to be no problem: teachers were simply recruited—usually cajoled or otherwise embarrassed into "volunteering"—from anyone who stepped through the church door, exhibited no acquaintance with the truth and reality of the gospel, was willing to help out the village folk, to be sure, yet who seemed not to have first-hand aquaintance with Jesus. The "born againers" ask us, "Do you have any confidence in the capacity of those people to provide Christian nurture for your child?"

It's regrettable whenever the conversation between these two groups spirals down into nastiness, for at this point neither party hears what the other is saying.

It's also regrettable when "born again" becomes a tool to secure political advantage. When Ronald Reagan was pursuing the presidency of the USA he advertised himself as "born again" for purely political reasons (it would help him garner votes) even though he didn't so much as go to church or display any interest in the faith.

Let's return to the two polarized parties. We're going to move beyond the polarization only as we recognize there to be as many ways of encountering Jesus Christ as there are ways of falling in love. To be sure, in matters of love some people are overwhelmed so as to be swept off their feet: "love at first sight" we call it. Despite the popularity of the *notion* of "love at first sight, the *fact* of it isn't common at all. Relatively few people fall in love "at first sight." Far more people find their relationship with someone they will eventually admit they love developing steadily, bit by bit, in a positive direction. Still others find that their coming to know someone else intimately is a much more drawn-out, up-and-down matter. Turbulent at times, it has to contend with dark moments and doubt, misunderstanding and confusion. But at the end of this up and down, hot and cold, now-ardent and then-distant undertaking there finally is resolution. And two people step ahead in a relationship that they will thereafter neither regret nor renounce.

Plainly it's false to maintain there's only one way of forging a most significant human relationship. Because false, it would also be silly to insist on "one way only." We don't question the authenticity of someone else's relationship because of the manner in which she arrived at it. We never say, "You can be in love now only if you came to be in love by the route we prescribe."

Then surely the polarization that arises within the church is overcome as we recognize that *how* someone comes to faith, by what route, isn't important at all; how someone comes to faith doesn't impugn the authenticity and integrity of her standing in Christ.

This is the first thing we should admit in our look at our Lord's encounter with Nicodemus: whatever the expression "born again" might mean, it doesn't mean that there is only one way of entering into and abiding in the company of Jesus Christ.

* * * * *

In the second place we must recognize that the life-transforming reality to which the expression points is something that everyone longs for. Or at least thoughtful people long for it, and so do wistful people, and more than a few desperate people.

The word in the text translated "again" or "anew" (*anothen*) has three meanings. It can mean "again" in the sense of "one more time;" that is, "again" in the sense of chronologically repeated. Or it can mean "from above;" that is, from the realm of the transcendent, from God. Or it can mean "from the beginning, a re-creation, with a new nature, a different nature."

Plainly Nicodemus fastens on the first meaning only, "one more time." "It's absurd," he says in so many words, "to suggest that a grown-up like me can enter his mother's womb one more time and repeat his physical extrusion." He's right: it *is* absurd.

But this first meaning of *anothen* is precisely what Jesus doesn't have in mind. Our Lord is thinking only of the latter two meanings: everyone may, and everyone should, be born from above, from God, and thereby be reborn with a new nature. Jesus maintains that life can begin anew; there can be a fresh beginning for everyone; we can begin again with a new nature, a different nature—and all of this a gift of grace from God's hand.

We saw earlier that everyone, deep down, longs for this, even if many of those who long for it despise the church, snicker at the gospel, and use the name of Jesus only to curse. Still, the endless religious pursuits to which people commit themselves tell us over and over everyone wants a fresh start that is more than a repetition of the "same old;" everyone wants a new beginning that is qualitatively new.

A television documentary featuring the wealthiest county of California informed viewers that this area leads the nation in the per capita purchase and use of hot tub baths, yoga, physical fitness zeal, transactional analysis, consumption of valium and self-help courses. The TV documentary made several trenchant points. One of them was this: the levels of unsatisfaction and frustration never decrease. Oasis after oasis turns out to be mirage. Everything that's supposed to advance people to the next level, a higher level, of "being" invariably fails to do so. None of the techniques, programmes or regimens appears to work.

Marin County, of course, is at bottom an intensification and magnification of the omnipresent longing to find a new factor in life that won't be merely one more factor but rather something that proves to be a genuine transformation of the whole of life. People want something that's going to make the profoundest difference. Thwarted, frustrated, irked, and now quietly desperate, people continue to grope. Many such people have admitted that they're jaded from trying new techniques and old panaceas, none of which delivers what it holds out. They're less certain of what they are looking for (if they knew precisely what they were looking for they'd also know where to look: the gospel) than they are certain of what they want to be rid of. "Marin County" happens to be everywhere.

At the same time that the earliest Christian community was adding daily those people who had come to know and enjoy what Jesus spoke of and delivered, Greek Mystery religions were seeking converts. In one of the rites of these Greek Mystery Religions the devotee, the "convert," stood in a pit that was covered with latticework. A bull was led onto the latticework. At the climax of the religious ceremony the bull's throat was slashed. As blood poured down, the devotee lifted her face and was bathed in blood. At this point the Mystery Religion priest pronounced her "reborn for eternity." Greek Mystery religion knew what it was to feel after something crucial; knew what it was to long for transformation of human existence. But Greek Mystery religion couldn't deliver the reality. What gave the earliest Christians their remarkable credibility was their ability to point with assurance to the One, Jesus Christ, who could deliver and did.

Apocalypse Now is an older movie that depicts the United States' conflict in Viet Nam. The movie portrays the contradictions that are part of any war. The movie ends with primitive Indo-Chinese backwoods folk ritually slaughtering bulls. The sword falls. The animal's head is severed. Blood spews. It sounds grotesque to the point of being nauseating. Yet the movie-scene doesn't appear to affect movie watchers in this way. Instead the scene rivets movie-watchers without sickening them. Plainly the scene speaks to something deep, something pre-conscious in the human psyche. The scene parallels the outlook of Greek Mystery religion 2000 years ago in at least one respect; namely, that the shedding of blood somehow, inexplicably, unpollutes the past, restores the present to sanity and integrity, and points to a new future that is genuinely "future" just because the "new" is genuinely new. Still, regardless of what is pointed to or felt after, the reality isn't delivered—whether at the hands of *Apocalypse Now* or Greek Mystery religion centuries ago.

The apostle John, however, possesses conviction born of his experience. For right in the midst of his account of our Lord's conversation with Nicodemus, John interjects the lifting up of Jesus, the blood-shedding of the Messiah. John knows that there is One whose blood *is* effectual, and there is One who *does* deliver what he holds out.

Regardless of how turned off people are by the glib use of "born again," there's no little evidence that all around us are people who long precisely for what Jesus holds out. Nicodemus, a mature, middle-aged man, and a member of the Sanhedrin, the highest religious council, came to Jesus under cover of darkness. What would a sophisticated fellow like him hope to gain from a thirty-year old peasant with sawdust in his hair, who came from a one-horse town, and whose contacts with religious leaders were consistently negative? What Nicodemus hoped to gain is what everyone longs for.

* * * * *

Even though he hopes to gain what he needs most, Nicodemus misunderstands Jesus' assertion. "Born again?" he asks, "It's physically impossible." All the while, of course, our Lord is talking about something different. While Jesus isn't speaking about physical birth, he's certainly using the analogy of physical birth.

Birth, everyday birth, is plainly a *change of context.* When a human being is born the context of that person's life changes from amniotic fluid to air; from confinement to freedom; from darkness to light; from silence to exclamation.

The kind of birth, "new birth," that Jesus speaks of in his conversation with Nicodemus is also a change of context: from spiritual inertia to spiritual vigour; from culpable ignorance of God to child-like wonder at God; from a human existence that prides itself on being self-sufficient to an existence that humbly thanks God for his condescension and grace. There's nothing un-understandable or cryptic about this. "You are a teacher of Israel and you don't understand this?" Jesus asks in genuine amazement. Surely Nicodemus ought to have understood this. After all, the presence and weight and force of the living God is the context in which Israel's life unfolds. God has made himself known to Israel in a way that he hasn't elsewhere, with the result that Israel's knowledge of God differentiates it from the surrounding nations. Israel has been given to know the One who creates life, moulds it, informs and directs and fulfils it. The prophets of Israel speak tirelessly of what it is to have life rooted in, informed by, and conformed to the God who acts upon his people and speaks to them in such a way that they know who he is and what he has done and what he requires of them. The prophets know that when God speaks to his people he quickens in them the capacity to respond and the desire to respond. Thereafter what we call "life" is life-long encounter with him who comes to us conclusively in Jesus Christ. Such intimacy means that we live henceforth in God, in a sphere, an atmosphere, whose reality is more vivid than the vividness of our five senses. It issues in new understanding, lively obedience, and profoundest contentment.

Surely there's nothing bizarre or spooky about this. When people today hear the words "born again," instantly they think of a highly unusual psychological development, an inner "trip" which they've never been on themselves and which they suspect in any case. Instead we should always remember that *birth means primarily change of context.* To have our lives unfold in the context or atmosphere of the living God is to live in an ongoing dialogue with God whose reality, simplicity, profundity is deeper than our language can describe.

"Too vague," someone objects. "All this change-of-context stuff; it's too nebulous." But it isn't vague. Those whom Jesus first called to himself didn't find him vague at all. Isn't the same Lord present to us now in his risen life? The faith of the church catholic is built on the assurance that he is. The saints of every age have known this. There's nothing vague here at all.

"Too presumptuous," someone else adds. But there's nothing presumptuous about someone who knows he's at the banquet by invitation only. The certainty that accompanies mercy-quickened faith has nothing to do with snobbish superiority. Those whom Jesus called didn't think they'd "arrived" in any sense. Still, they were certain that they were on the right road and didn't need to look for any other.

"Too narrow," someone insists; "It reeks of religious sentimentality, a nostalgia-trip unrelated to life." It would be sentimental only if it promoted maudlin slovenliness. It would be unrelated to life only if were a private trip that had nothing to do with everyday matters. But in fact it has everything to do with every aspect of life.

Birth always means change of context. To be born again, born anew, born from above is to encounter God and thereafter live with him in a dialogue wherein we know our sin pardoned, our way in life made plain (plain, not easy), our hearts encouraged and our minds informed and our wills fortified.

* * * *

In light of the understanding we've gained we should move beyond a polarization that helps no one. We should acknowledge that how one comes to faith, or how long one takes to come to faith, is beside the point.

We should admit that there's a persistent and profound spiritual hunger in people all around us. And in word and deed we should point to him who is that context in which all of life is transfigured, and who has manifestly transformed our lives as well.

"Heavenly things," we ought always to remember, have everything to do with our earthliness.